AF597474

sumdumhonky

Lloyd Price

Published by
Cool Titles
439 N. Canon Dr., Suite 200
Beverly Hills, CA 90210
www.cooltitles.com

The Library of Congress Cataloging-in-Publication Data Applied For

Lloyd Price—
sumdumhonky

p. cm
ISBN 978-1-935270-35-5
1. Musician Memoir 2. African American History 3. Civil Rights
I. Title
2015

Printed in the United States of America

1 3 5 7 9 10 8 6 4 2

Book editing and design by White Horse Enterprises, Inc.

For interviews or information regarding special discounts for bulk purchases, please contact cindy@cooltitles.com

Distribution to the Trade: Pathway Book Service,
www.pathwaybook.com, pbs@pathwaybook.com, 1-800-345-6665

DEDICATION

In memory of all who contributed
to the destruction of my innocence.

Table of Contents

Acknowledgments

First let me say thanks. I'm deeply indebted to all who have believed in me and my music. I'll always be grateful for that. Special thanks to my fans worldwide for their support all these years. Music went through many changes socially and I am so proud that my music still stands. Thank you to the youth and the youth movement that came from my music.

I'd also like to thank my mother, Beatrice, and father, Louis, for putting up with me as I was trying to find my way, and discover who I was. When I was young I believed I could be just as good as anybody else and could make a difference in the world. What made that so was that I believed in music—not knowing how big a difference I could really make.

All of the grace, however goes to my heroes: my wife Jacqueline for her steadfastness and loyalty; Louis Jordan, Charles Brown, Joe Louis, Roscoe Garden, Amos Milburn, T. Bone Walker, Roy Milton, Nellie Lutcher, Buddy and Ella Johnson, Ruth Brown, and the Liggins Brothers, all of whom

I listened to in my mother's fish shop, and danced to their music. Mr. Morgan in Kenner, Louisiana, my hometown, gave me the opportunity with my first little band to play on Friday nights. He gave me a chance to play the piano with my brother Leo on drums and get me started. None of this could've happened if not for him. Thanks also to Dave Bartholomew for being in Kenner on that day and thinking I had talent on that old piano when I had the radio on listening to Okey Dokey Smith, my first black disc jockey. I loved him and that's where I discovered what "personality" was.

I want to thank Ol' Jake, too, for all the pain and harassment he caused me. He didn't know it, but through him I was able to see the world like it was, and find the strength to see that he was no better than I was. He gave me courage to believe I could be better, and never want to be the kind of person he was. His abuse drove me to the point where I, without knowing it, changed the sound of music forever. I did that by running away from people like Jake in my mind. May his soul rest in peace. Finally, many thanks to the town of Kenner, Louisiana for naming the street I grew up on after me, Lloyd Price Avenue. It's where old Jake used to chase me. Miracles do happen.

Introduction

I was born March 9, 1933 in Kenner, Louisiana, which was about as southern a place as anyone could be here in the United States. There are places farther south, but no place is more southern in its thought and attitude than Kenner.

A big part of the thinking by the people who ran the town of Kenner in the 1930s and 1940s (all white people by the way) assumed that black people were nothing. No, that's not quite right, they thought black people were less than nothing. They thought dogs were better than people of color. I guess I shouldn't say all white people in the town thought that way, but as you will read, every white person I knew there did, and they had many ways of showing how they felt.

What self-esteem I have, I got from my parents and extended family. My mother, Beatrice, was the leader of our pack and very strong. She was my motivation, with her strong drive and attitude. There were eight boys and three girls in our family: Alfred, Herman, Elbridge, Louis Jr., Julius, Mildred, Rose Mary, Lloyd, Leo, Charles, and Barbara.

I was eighth in the line-up. Our mother had a house full and she didn't mess around. When I say she was in charge, that's what I mean. Even though all of us weren't always there at the same time, you'd never believe the way she worked that little six-room house at 323 Butler Street, which was not too far from where the New Orleans airport is now. Forever, my mother will always have my respect.

Our mother was always afraid of losing one of us. If any of us went out, her biggest fear was that we might not come back. Strange things happened to black people in the South then, and our mother knew if we didn't come home we'd be lost forever. No one would look for us, as a missing black person was no concern of the law then. That's the way things were. We depended on each other. We had nothing and no one else but us. The way things were, if some white man didn't speak for a black person, they were a lost soul.

When I was young, it was driven into our heads by both our parents that there would come a time when the world would be a better place. This was, of course, if we were lucky enough to survive, and to escape the gowned white men in long black cars. "Make sure they don't catch you," we were told. "Stay alert and be aware of your fears. If you should see them, run, and turn that fear into strength." I guess I adopted my mother's fearlessness and courage, because in my heart I never fully accepted the conditions of that time, and I survived.

My mother had a restaurant called Beatrice's Fish 'n' Fry. This was in spite of all the many things she had to do with eleven children in the course of her day. She found time to run a business, keep all of us on track, work for the town doctor, and be my father's wife.

My father, Louis, was a simple, hard-working man, but he was humble and meek when it came to the running of our home. He loved his wife and his eleven children, just as we all loved each other. He was a longshoreman, but my mother's job was much tougher. As can you imagine, owning a restaurant was an eighteen-hour workday. When my dad came home, his day was over, but not hers. She worked way into the night trying to make things better for our family. My mother's whole life was in the kitchen cooking, or in the washroom washing clothes (or both), until bedtime. She did this just to make ends meet.

Growing up wasn't easy when I was a boy, but I always loved singing and dancing. People often threw nickels and dimes on the floor just to see me work it. I also learned to play trumpet and piano because of my love for the sound of music. I thought it was great when my older brother Julius went on his way to do military service in the coast guard, because he gave me his trumpet.

Back then I was alone in thinking that, one day, I would hear myself on the jukebox. I also can't remember not having the dream of finding a way out of Kenner. That was the driving motivator behind my musical dreams: getting a bus ticket and leaving town. Somehow, I always knew the ticket would come from my love of music.

Not once did I ever think my way out would be from church—and it wasn't. I never sang in church. There were a lot of great gospel singers at the time, but I was never one of them. It actually never crossed my mind. To me, with my thoughts and what was in my heart, singing gospel would have been hypocritical. I was taught not to ever play with God, and I wasn't going to mess that up by mixing my singing together with religion. There was no way I would put God in the middle and have my dream shattered, so I taught myself to play piano.

From there I ended up being America's first black teen idol, and the first rock star of the 1950s, black or white. Over the years my music and career brought me many things, including that bus ticket I had dreamed of for so long. And, all over the world I was allowed to spread joy as a musical pioneer. I have also been able to bring youth of all colors together with my music. I even brought music to groups that had never spoken to each other, music with a new sound we now know as rock and roll. I still find it amazing that youth came together all because of a sound.

You might remember a few of my songs: "Lawdy Miss Clawdy" (1952), "Stagger Lee," (1959), and "Personality" (1959). These songs started the youth movement of the early 1950s, and bloomed across America and around the world. Kids had never before bought records like they bought "Lawdy Miss Clawdy." That song changed the way people listened to music. And because of music, because of rock and roll, the world has never been the same.

White record stores had never sold race music before, but were now selling it from under the counter. Eventually they sold it from bins and racks, above and across the counter. Today, "Lawdy Miss Clawdy" has been recorded more than 178 times by the biggest recording stars in the world, including such diverse artists as Elvis Presley, Joe Cocker, Paul McCartney, The Beatles, and Little Richard. I've had more than twenty-five albums, and more than thirty charted singles on the *Billboard* Pop and R&B charts. I say this to tell you if a little black kid from Kenner, Louisiana was told by white people all his life that he was nothing can accomplish that, what can *you* get done?

Thank goodness times have changed since I was born more than eighty years ago. Blacks can now drink from the same water fountain as white people, eat at the same restaurants, ride in the front on public transportation, get a bank loan, hold jobs in management—and we don't get lynched quite as often as we used to. But, prejudice still exists, more in some people and places than others. It is still here.

I wrote the essays in this book to empower you, the reader. Each essay has a different flavor, a unique style, and is about a pivotal time in my life. I also wanted to remind everyone, no matter what his or her color, where we were sixty, seventy, eighty years ago. Ten years ago. And, where we are today. I also have had some amazing experiences along the way that I hope you'll learn something from. I know I did.

For example, when I left Kenner there was one black policeman, but he was not allowed to carry a gun or arrest white people. Then there was Ol' Jake, a white policeman who could not read his name if he saw it written in the sky. He didn't even have sense enough to know how to spell the names of the two guns he carried. And he called black folks dumb. But, look what's happening. Today we have a black president who has his trigger finger on the power of the world. They've named the cross street behind my childhood home Lloyd Price Avenue. Why, in 1998, I was even inducted into the Rock & Roll Hall of Fame. I wonder what Ol' Jake would have to say about that.

Time brings about change, and the change of my generation was about one thing: music. It brought people together like nothing had ever before. One other thing is true. It wasn't just here in America that the curse of racism existed. If you had a black face you found prejudice everywhere: Japan, Africa, France, England, Germany, and many other places. There wasn't anywhere in the world where I didn't find prejudice, so I chose to take it as a blessing, not an insult. The black face is the black man, so I'm blessed and thankful that God wanted me to be seen.

And, I'm thankful for my music, for it has brought the world's people together. I know there are some who may question this fact, but some histories don't lie, and this is one of them.

You also may have questions about the title of book, *sumdumhonky*. It refers to being brought up in the South as a black child. That was no picnic with the whites in charge, and a piece of my life in Africa was no holiday either, as you will learn. The title represents a feeling of a time gone by, of a past that needs to be remembered, and many cruel white men who thought they ruled the world. Perhaps you never experienced what I have. If so, God has blessed you, but I hope you'll remember my experiences, so that no one in the future has to endure the same tragedies and humiliations.

Lloyd Price
November 2014

1
Who Feared Whom

When I was a boy growing up in the Deep South I used to wonder why all the black people I knew thought the white man was so smart. And, if we were to believe the white man, why all black people were dumb. Today, I still wonder why on earth we believed that. Was it our inner fear of the white man that made us believe he had a monopoly on brainpower? We were all poor, black and white, just plain folk, bunched up together in that little Louisiana town of Kenner, trying to find our way. We all had nothing, and were all thrown together in a little country place west of New Orleans with a lot of dusty roads.

What was it that made the white man think his life had more value than ours? Was it the inferior education that he allowed us to have in that little wet, cold room we called the black school? Classes were always over-crowded, and it was one school for all grades from one though twelve. Each teacher also had to teach more than one class. The first class might have been grade one taught by a particular teacher and the next class was grade nine, taught by the same teacher. It was such a strain on the teachers and the students that it wasn't possible for any of us to learn anything.

The white man knew we couldn't beat him in schooling, so he set the trap. We all knew it too, because he gave us the books to read, and page after page it was all about him. There was nothing about the black man in those books, no history, as if he never existed. Why?

And why didn't he like us? Was it because we were poor black folk that he took advantage of us, or because the law was on his side? We had no way to defend ourselves or even know what the truth was. Seriously, what was the truth? Back then we had no voice, and I mean *none*. Two friends of mine, A-Jones and E-Saw, were so afraid of white men they truly thought they walked on water, just like Jesus did.

As a child, I had great fear that the white man would hurt me. Why? Because of the extreme power he had over us. My fear also stemmed from the fact that my dad had undying respect and fear of "the man." I knew a white man would sooner shoot me as speak to me. I learned that early on and all of us believed it. My life is filled with questions I'll never know the answers to, but having had eight decades to reflect without getting shot, I still wonder.

There was a time when black people were afraid of a passing hearse, or of a nun or priest in black. This was because as children, we learned that black was a dirty word. So if the white man was a god and the color black was dirty, why was the priest wearing it? It was all so confusing. I had never seen a black priest. Even now I don't know if there were any black priests back then. I did know when I was young that blacks couldn't go to the white Catholic church in our town.

Yep, that's the way it was in my hometown of Kenner, Louisiana. The white man ruled the rural South, and at the same time called himself a God-fearing man. You never would've thought so, the way he treated black people. There was a population of about 500 people in town then, and I can't honestly say what the mix between black and white was, but my parents told us to listen when the white man spoke.

"Don't ever talk back if you don't want trouble," they said. "If a white person ever shows up at our house, know that he is there with trouble on his mind. If he says he wants to talk to you, it isn't because he is being friendly, it is because of something he heard that you did, or saw you do, and he is going to chastise you. He never shows up for a neighborly conversation."

I was about nine years old—or maybe a bit younger—when I became truly aware of "him." My feelings for the white man at that time etched in my heart my complete distrust. The reason I've held on to the memory is there was one white man in particular who feared me the most, and who I feared.

Kenner, Louisiana was a one-horse town where everybody knew everybody, black or white. We were all cousins. The man named Ol' Jake was no exception, but he was extraordinary. I mentioned in the introduction that the whole town knew Ol' Jake was about the dumbest white man in the parish, and yet he had guns. If you paid him, he couldn't put five words together in a sentence, but whenever there was a group of us black kids, he was always the first one to make fun of us.

If we walked past him, Ol' Jake always shouted, "All y-you ni-ni-niggas go-go back to Aa-a-africa." He stuttered so bad it was hard to understand him, but he always managed to get that out. And his words always left us with questions. What is Africa? Where is it? Where should we go back to? In that regard Ol' Jake knew something we didn't. Somebody had told him that Africa was a place where black folks came from. No one had ever told me that, or maybe I wasn't listening. The Africa I had heard about was a jungle, and nobody came from there. According to my teacher, Africa was where little pig-men who looked like black people and who ate each other lived. It wasn't until much later in my life that I realized my teacher had been talking about Pygmies.

"You don't want ever want to go to Africa," my teacher said, "because people there are only half human."

So when Ol' Jake said "go back to Africa," it hurt worse than being called a nigger, because what he really meant was that we were just half human. That hurt, especially because there were no adults around to defend us. Were we really just half human, my young boy's mind wondered? Is that why he said that?

One day, as kids do, I was riding my bike on the road and an old police car pulled up behind me. Guess who was in it? It was Ol' Jake in a police uniform.

"Hey bo-boy. D-don't be ri-ridin' d-dat bike so-so, c-c-close to der ro-road. I'm a dern-new po-lice, d-don't ask me t-to arrest ya."

When you're young a lot of things don't hit you right away, but even so, at that moment, everything in me felt something was wrong with Ol' Jake having a gun and wearing a police uniform. He probably got no pay for the job. His services could have been free, just the privilege of having a gun was probably enough for him. That and the right to talk to and do black folk anyway he saw fit. Even though he might have thought that *we* thought he walked on water, what we really thought was that he should have gotten in it. That smelly man needed a bath!

One night word got around that Ol' Jake had killed Walter King. Everybody knew Walter, a young-ish black man whose mind was strange. Nobody took Walter seriously, whatever he said or did. Rumor had it that Jake shot Walter because he had talked back to him.

"He gave me some lip so I shot him," Ol' Jake bragged later. Even if Walter did talk back, who gave Ol' Jake that God-like power to take someone's life, just because he was talked back to?

Was it the sheriff of our town who gave Ol' Jake the authority to take a life because he didn't like what was said? That question was valid. I also couldn't figure out why our sheriff had a gun either. He, too, had problems thinking he had a special arrangement with God. The sheriff was the town's everything man for all white folks, and a nigger beater who I heard often preached in church, "the best nigger is a dead one." One fact was as plain as the skin on my face: it was no secret about his feelings toward people of color.

Is that why our sheriff kept getting appointed? Because he believed he'd earned special points with God? This man was sheriff before I was old enough to speak my name, and he was still sheriff when I left town. They said he had a wooden leg and was half blind in one eye. Was that reason to make him believe he was special? Or, was it because he'd shot so many black folk that even the white people had lost count? Was that why he thought he'd earned special recognition from God?

With all those reappointments to the office of sheriff, and with a blessing and reward for a job well done, nobody around our part of town had ever seen anyone like him. There were some things said about him and his cruelty toward people of color, but the older generation was afraid to say anything negative. And, since colored folks were discouraged from voting at the time, I have to think his reappointments were because of his control over helpless old people through the claim of law and order. I imagine it wasn't that difficult to get the nod from the good old, bald-headed boys club, but people of color had no influence, no voice, no power.

Why would you give a coward a gun, no matter what his size? After each reappointment the sheriff's head swelled to the size of a watermelon. Politics really do make strange bedfellows. Hatred toward anyone other than white people made our sheriff popular, and a hero with the majority—the white majority. He also had a big, ten-gallon hat to go with his big ego and his big gun.

Our sheriff was also notorious for surrounding himself with family and friends. All had guns, it was later found out, because most of them were members of the same club, the "Klan." Back in the 1930s, the Ku Klux Klan flourished in the southern part of the United States. They all wore white robes and conical hoods that were designed to scare, and also hide the wearer's identity. But everybody knew who they were when the members terrorized black people. Victims would not say specifically who each person was, but it was well known among us who they were, as we knew each member well, from the sheriff's office to the church.

In all honesty, it didn't take an election, a wearing of the hood, or a membership in the "club." If you were white, it was all right to carry a gun. And speaking of guns, it didn't take much to qualify for one—if you were white. All you needed was a cousin or a friend. Even knowing the sheriff was enough.

I'm still trying to figure out why the sheriff allowed Ol' Jake to carry a gun when if Ol' Jake stopped you on the road you'd have to write your own ticket. Jake would have to ask you to sign the ticket for him. You could write "Superman," or "Kiss my ass, Jake." He'd never know the difference.

Knowing how stupid he was, for entertainment, we kids used to make him chase us. He had a big fat ass and weighed at least three hundred pounds. He also always had a wad of chewing tobacco or snuff stuffed in his mouth, so there was no way he could ever catch us. "Yer lil' bla-black nigga ba-ba-bastards," he'd stammer. "I'm a gonna g-git yer."

It was great fun for us, but looking back, we weren't so smart either. That asshole had a gun. It wasn't so funny on Sundays either, when we came home from Sunday school and had to pass Ol' Jake and his buddies. When me and some buddies saw them, they were always at a little watchman tower at the railroad track crossing.

There was a nasty little game Ol' Jake and his friends played: who could spit tobacco juice the farthest. But, when we got near them, they would start farting to see who could do it the loudest, and then grab one of us and say we did it. They'd stand to block our path and laugh their asses off. We were scared half to death because we didn't know what they might do next. Sometimes they'd grab one of our hands and hold it to their ass and laugh while they farted on it and scream, "Boy, spot that!" This is what they called having fun: scaring little boys who were just eight and nine years old.

These were the town's lawmen, our sheriff and Ol' Jake. They had guns and, yes, I feared them. Jake's mind was warped. We knew "sick" would be a better word for him, as he'd go out and shoot up road signs, and then blame it on the coloreds so he'd have somebody to harass or arrest.

It was no secret about how Ol' Jake loved shooting rabbits, and anything else that couldn't shoot back, just to hurt it. My dad said if the rabbit could throw a rock back there'd be less people hunting him. Maybe we should've listened, because Ol' Jake loved shooting anything that wouldn't fight back. It seemed as if he killed solely for the sake of seeing blood and smelling gunpowder.

What freaked me out was that blacks weren't supposed to know the difference between smart and dumb, or good or bad, yet we knew who all of the hooded men were, and we knew their nature, hooded or not. These men had absolutely no respect for a person of color, even if the black man weighed 500 pounds and was seven feet tall with a Ph.D. from Yale. It didn't matter. If you were black you just didn't count. And, Ol' Jake aside, what was so ridiculous was that if you wrote any of these "smart" guy's names, they couldn't read it.

If you were white, being literate and intelligent were certainly not qualifications for the job of sheriff. All you needed to be was white and you were qualified—especially if you were like Ol' Jake. I talk about Jake and the sheriff, but they were not alone in their thinking. In addition to the restaurant, my mother worked for the town's doctor. Can you imagine the kind of treatment we got from him? We had no choice but to go to him when we were sick, as there was no such thing as a black doctor in our town.

It never ceases to amaze me how people like the sheriff, Ol' Jake, and the doctor always knew when to hide if danger arose—and how little they really knew about us. When I was young the white man seemed to trust us more than he did his own family. Maybe that tells you who was dumb and who was smart? He trusted us with his food. We bought it, cleaned it, and cooked it, but couldn't sit at the same table with him to eat it. We poured his drinks, but he didn't have a clue what was in it. He trusted us with his kids, in some cases from tits to teens, then he told them not to socialize with us because we were beneath them. Yet all their lives this white man and his family ate from the same black hands that cooked his food and drink. Ain't that a bitch?

I was confused and intimidated by this kind of white man most of my youth, but then I began to realize that he was just sumdumhonky. It came to me one day that this white man was far from being smart—at least not about black people. We cook his food and he can't stand us?

Most of the white men in the area thought they were something other than what they were. Playing with matches and burning sticks in the shape of a cross in the dark, for them that was a big idea. But that was okay, as long as he believed he was smarter than the black man. I wonder what is it like to spend your whole day thinking about what you could do to harm or frighten someone else and their family? I know all of the terror in Kenner was not a one-man think tank. How many beers and shots of whiskey do you think it took for a bunch of cowards to get enough nerve to go hang a helpless black man?

When I was a kid I got tired of hearing that one of us was missing. There was a lot of bragging at the railroad track crossing about shooting a "nigger" out of a tree on Sundays. Ol' Jake wasn't the only one who had "fun" on that day. No, white folk used Sunday day as a family fun day and what could be better fun than chasing and treeing a nigger after church? If the crowd was big enough, there was a good chance that the one who caused the most pain would get an appointment for some kind of office in the parish.

Isn't it pathetic that with all the hurt and suffering our sheriff caused, not once did any black person ever wait behind a bush to harm him. We knew where to find him, especially on Sunday when he was in church on his knees with his bible clutched in his hands lying to God and singing about how much he loved Jesus and his fellow Christians, and to fight onward as a Christian soldier. Is that what a Christian is, and what he stands for? Inflict as much pain as possible on other humans?

As you can see, growing up I was filled with conflict because it was the white people who set the standard in our town for everything. How could they hate us so much and then go to church and preach love? How could my family be on their knees working and begging for help, and get leftovers, old clothes, and small change for pay, and the Christian, the white man, believed he was good to us? Why did the white man think he deserved to be a wingman for the angels in heaven when he died?

The black man was surely heading for hell, if there is such a place. That's what I was always told. But I thought that if God's duty was to take the white man in with wings of reward, then hell had to be a better place for me. How could anyone believe in God, like this man says he does, and not believe in any of God's other creations? That's impossible for me to conceive and hard to believe. And how was it that God created only the white man as an equal to him?

It had to be that moonshine the white man was drinking when he left church, thinking he was blessed just for being there. He had some of that brewed moonshine and got drunk, drunk enough to temper his spirit, and if by chance he saw one of us little black kids he'd rise up and damn near break his foot trying to kick our little asses. Then he'd say the devil made him do it. And he just told God that he holds no hatred for any man, because he was an onward Christian soldier.

We had no power, no land, no banks, no religion of our own, but the white man must have sensed something or known something we didn't. Remember, white men like him wrote the good book. Being black in the South back then, when "god" spoke, or even when his name was mentioned, there were two things you did. You feared him and you listened.

All that stuff the white man preached of truth and sorrow. Did the white man really think he could bullshit God? I often wondered what Ol' Jake would've done if he ever saw a young white woman with a black man. That would have been something! He'd probably have gotten up off his knees thinking God had betrayed him and never go back to church again.

"Imagine God letting a nigger hold hands with a white woman when God himself is a white man?" Ol' Jake might have thought. "Surely this is a mistake. God is more sensitive than that, and to true his messengers. How can He betray him for a nigger?"

Not the God he prayed to, of course. No, that God was on his side. I can see Ol' Jake now after feeling betrayed, tearing up the private phone number, the one he said God gave him. It makes me wonder if he's had that conversation yet. Why did God, with all His infinite wisdom, allow black and white to mix, Jake might have asked. Why didn't He keep it pure?

Seems like all those southern white men thought God was theirs and theirs alone. He couldn't understand, because he believed "God created man in his own image" and he wasn't no nigger. That was something he believed strongly. Every time he looked at that picture, at that white painting of The Last Supper by Michelangelo, he believed it.

I can't imagine my God making me put my hand on a book (written and published by people like Ol' Jake, and a tool used to kill many thousands of people over the centuries) to worship him, and making somebody like me believe it's the truth. Above all, there's nothing else the white man wants than for me to swear on top of it. Can you imagine?

Show me anywhere in the bible where it speaks of a black man or black woman being an angel, or even as an aide in His heaven. Let me say here that I'm a strong believer in my faith and its power of the unknown. I'm very clear about those who walked the earth, as I do now, and the stories they told. My proof is in the amazing secrets of the unknown. My faith is in seeing the changing seasons, flying birds, running rivers, and endless creatures with names we don't yet know, the mysteries that seem to have no end. That's the wonder of the God I know.

Here's a question and a perspective from someone who grew up in the Deep South. Why do white people rush to the sun to look like us? Do they want to have a kind and peace-loving soul, as we do? Do they want to be the kind of people we are, people who are happy just being a child of this great soil? Is that why the white man, a man like Ol' Jake, wants to change his color? Why are black people reviled for their color, yet white people who sit in the sun and get tan are seen as having a high status?

Ol' Jake couldn't be happy with us, and couldn't live without us, and keeping that buried deep in his heart made him mad as hell. Could it be fear that made him and others who wore sheets and white hoods over their face and played with fire in the night, burning the cross they swear by, the one thing he said he'd die to defend? Where is his truth? How brave is this earthly man who likens himself to God? Is he the brave white hunter who sits on top of an eight-ton elephant ten feet above ground with a thirty-thirty rifle in his hands? Or is the brave one the little African boy on the ground who leads the elephant though the jungle with a stick in his hand, looking for the lions. They say a picture is worth a thousand words, and that would be a very special picture.

It's true that memory goes everywhere you go, even into death. Ol' Jake's probably been dead more than fifty years. If he's still living then he must have some personal contact with God, but wherever he is, pleasant memories. R.I.P. Jake. You can't change the fact that no matter what you thought about us, it was always what we thought about you that counted.

▲

Things today aren't anywhere near as bad as they used to be with the white man in the South, but even now some of those chilling experiences from the past creep up on me. Sometimes just being in an elevator with a white man, and seeing the way he looks at me, lets me know the white man of my past is still there, watching and waiting.

I was in a London hotel not long ago, in the elevator, and there was a guy in the elevator with me, an American. You had to have a key to get to the floor I was on, and so did he. When I put my key in the same lock for the suites floor as he did, I thought he was going to crap in his pants. To see his face turn so red, it was hard not to feel sorry for him.

Some white men still think we actually believe it was *he* who created heaven and earth. All the power and privilege over people of color is his. Is that something I feel from the past? No, it is still very present today. Many times I feel it, even in a cab or a department store. Like I don't belong. Yes, he's still out there. You can feel his eyes. A black person has to watch how he is looked over in public places, as if he was invisible just by being a person of color. Pay attention.

If you took note of this white man's ways, you'd find him acting like a direct descendant of God, as if all he has to do is pick up a phone and talk to Him on His private line, just like Ol' Jake. There are no limits with this kind of white man, especially when he looks down his nose at you and preaches about wrong and right. Pay attention and watch him when he sings "God Bless America." Is he singing about himself?

One day when I was a grown man I was at a ball game and I watched a white man sing "The Battle Hymn of the Republic." Tears flooded his eyes as he hugged his bible as if it was his first-born child. It made me wonder if he really was God's messenger, with all his sincerity.

For decades, every time I turned around it seemed there was a white man right there to tell me I didn't know nothing, that a nigger and a monkey had the same intellect. That's why even at a young age of fifteen I knew for sure that Kenner, Louisiana was not the place I wanted to be. So, my first opportunity was my last, and I have never gone back.

2
How My Life Was Changed

I would venture to say that most of the young black men of my generation didn't have very much to dream about. Things were getting better, but it was no picnic living in the Deep South. We had our one and only hero, fighter Joe Louis, and we all wanted to be like him. He was our big, picture window to the outside world, but we knew most of us would never get there. The next best thing from our point of view was to go into the segregated army, or become a Pullman porter on the train.

It was okay. Young black men of my generation didn't have much by way of hope, but what we had was a loving family and each other. After World War II, though, we were given the opportunity to go to school, to college, even though it was late. Most white kids our age were already going to college, but a young black man's first choice was to work and help support his family, so most of us let the privilege of education go by. Through the eyes of our older brothers, and our fathers who had traveled and seen things, we did realize that education, however we could get it, was a good thing. Education was important, but the needs of the family had to come first, so it was a job over school.

By the end of the war, our mothers and sisters were also no longer doing Miss Sadie's housework. They now had factory jobs and other kinds of work choices. And the white people we knew seemed a little more civil after the war. I began thinking: was the America I had known the same place?

Even at our house at the dinner table there were no more slaps on the head for wanting seconds at dinner. Things were looking up. And beside our own brothers, there were other people's brothers from our town who had gone into the service and overseas, and who gave us the pleasure of their stories about the war and the ways of the world in far away places. They also told us about the different kinds people who lived there. As I listened, I'd visualize myself being there, and my vision was so strong I could actually feel it. With every beat of my heart I knew I would someday see the world. What a wonderful time I had inside my head, trying to make sense of it all when I listened to those stories. They were so different from the world I knew and lived in.

I was willing to bet my dad had never crossed the state line out of Louisiana, as he had no stories to tell us other than how to work. There were times he'd come home from work and all he could do was sit on the porch swing and smoke his pipe. I always thought he was trying to find a way to relax, just so he could breathe before he ate. I remember telling myself that I never wanted to be like that. To me, Dad seemed to be a person who was lost, a man without any vision of moving forward. I always felt pain in my heart for him and desperately wanted to find a way to help. I guess I knew way back then at the age of nine that I didn't want to be like my father.

I don't recall exactly when it happened, but I believe I was somewhere between ten and eleven years old when my father broke his hip on the job. He was a longshoreman at the time and I believe he was a crane operator on one of those big banana boats that came from Cuba to New Orleans. It was an extraordinary job for a black man then. He'd been able to buy a bigger house for us, six rooms, and he and my mother were doing well until that ax came down and he could no longer work. Dad was laid up for months, not able to walk, and with my older brothers in the service I was the oldest able-bodied male child in the house. Of my two older sisters, one was in school and the other was pregnant and about to get married.

I will never forget the day my mother came home from work looking very tired; the day that unbeknownst to me was the day that would change my life forever. Then she asked me to come sit close beside her.

"Son," she said, tears in her eyes. "Your father is down, and it's getting very hard for me to keep going. I know you're in school but I need some help. With your brothers in the service and getting married, I can't expect help from them. You are now big enough, so we're going to have to find a way to keep you going to school while you find some work."

Besides loving my mother and father (they were truly my heroes), it was heartwarming to know that my mother could confide in me, to tell me she couldn't do it alone, and needed my help. Even at that age I was feeling grown. I could see things were deteriorating, and it broke my heart because our parents had worked so hard for us.

Then, with no idea of what I was saying, and begging my mother not to cry, I told her I would find work.

True to my word when the iceman, Mr. Joe, came the next morning, I asked him did he need any help, because I would like a job.

"Son," he asked, "how much do you weigh?"

"I don't know, sir," I said.

"You don't look like a heavy weight, but I guess you can carry twenty-five pounds of ice. I do need somebody. Old Cool Breeze didn't show up this morning. Did your mother say it was okay for you to work?"

"Oh, yes sir," I said excitedly, "she wants me to work so I can help out."

"Okay," he said. "Go tell her you're going with me. I'm going to pay you fifty cents a morning, and I'll pick you up every morning. You'll work from at six A.M. to eight-thirty. That way you can be in school by nine. Okay?"

"Yes sir," I said, and I was as happy as any ten-year-old could be.

At first I thought working on the ice truck would be a snap, that it would be fun and easy, but boy was I wrong. Jumping on and off that sucker from six to eight-thirty was a job within itself. When I got to school I was always tired and never had my homework, but I was helping at home and that's what counted. I was making twenty-five cents per hour, and the grown ups at the sawmill were only getting thirty-five, so I had to keep that job.

And that's how my new life began. I worked for Mr. Joe on the ice truck in the morning and racked pins at the bowling alley in the evening after school. Whatever little boy thoughts I had left me that first day. I once had hopes to be somebody who flew airplanes. But, my hope of becoming the first black airplane pilot was gone from the first time I ever saw a plane in the sky. I told my mother that's what I wanted to do and she said that was not for colored people.

Actually, after my first day on the ice job, everything I thought as a kid was gone—and never came back. When I started to work, I began to see myself as the man of the house. I vowed to do whatever I could to help my mother and father, because it seemed like he wasn't getting any better. Something had gone wrong in the healing process and his hip had to be broken again so it could heal right.

In the meantime, I'd gotten yet another job, fixing flats and washing cars at Mr. Ike's filling station on the weekends. I liked that better than the job at the bowling alley. The tips were better and on school days I worked four hours, from four to eight P.M. In doing that, school became less and less important, but I kept going.

There was an old piano in our house, and no matter where I turned when I was not at work or at school, it kept calling my name. For a while I thought I might be losing it, or that the house was haunted, because that piano kept calling. I really couldn't play it. Half the keys were broken, or sticking, but I couldn't pass it by. On days my mother allowed me to stay home from school, I invariably found myself sitting on the stool picking at the keys. The piano had always been there and I had never been interested in it, but all of a sudden it just seemed to command my attention.

As time went on my teacher noticed I was coming to school in wet clothes, and that I was coming late. She asked what was going on and I told her I had to work because my father had broken his hip. I also told her the reason I'd fall asleep on my desk was that I was up so early every morning. Apparently, my answer was not acceptable.

My teacher took me to the principal's office and I suppose it was then I discovered I didn't really like school. They had no way of knowing this and I didn't either, until then, because whatever they decided, I didn't feel anything. The principal said I needed to try to do better in my class or I might fail. Little did they know my interest had grown more and more in the direction of that old piano. It kept telling me something, and I believed I could play it. My interest was in helping my parents, not in school, and for some reason I believed the piano was the way to do it. Nothing was going to stop me from trying to help them, and it was then that I chose a new direction.

I will never forget my parents and will love them always. Also, I believe it was their faith in me that drove me to that old piano. I loved my dad, and loved when he had time to hum and chant old songs. Boy did he have soul! In that sense I guess I'm a lot like him. As the old saying goes, the apple doesn't fall far from the tree. Despite his injury, I remember him doing everything he could for his family, and for whoever else he could help.

He loved going to church, because he believed and trusted in the Word. But when he broke his hip, his church members were slow in coming to help. It was as though he'd never done anything for anyone, and I think that hurt him deeply. It's a funny thing about Christianity, it seems like it's a wellness club—as long as you can donate all is well. But, if one gets sick, all you get is a prayer.

Dad's progress in healing could not have been slower. It seemed as though he was never going to get any better and

I would be stuck doing these little jobs forever, as we had no help from our church. After two years of carrying ice, and fixing flats, and racking pins, I developed into a good size for my age. I had a friend, John, who told me if I went to the big new airport that wasn't too far from our house, I might get a job in the kitchen at Dobbs House Restaurant. That way I could give up the ice truck and fixing those big ass truck tires at Mr. Ike's.

I went out there and got hired on the spot. I thought I was in heaven because I saw more food in that kitchen than I could eat in my entire life. And, instead of making fifty cents a morning with Mr. Joe, plus the little money I made fixing flats, I was now making twenty-six dollars and forty cents a week. I had never heard of so much money!

During the few odd hours I was at home, and for reasons still unknown to me, I was beginning to learn how to play that old piano. One day while picking on the keys, my little brother, Leo, brought out a cardboard beer case, and sat down beside me and began beating on it with a stick. At the time I didn't know the real function of a drummer, but Leo had rhythm, and it gave me what I now know as timing. And wouldn't you know, before God got the news, we had the hottest little teenage band around.

That's when school became fun again. Instead of having lunch, Leo and I found ourselves in the music room with the piano making what we called music (although the teachers called it noise). I had no idea what we were doing, but I should have taken notice. All the kids came to hear us, as they had never seen any thing like us. Soon we were the talk around school. Can you imagine? I was called a piano player! I knew all of three chords.

In the meantime, my dad still couldn't work and my mom depended on me more and more. Somewhere along in here I was beginning to wish I was older, so I could join the army and make more money to help them. It never crossed my mind that I could one day get paid for playing the piano. Then a club owner named Mr. Morgan, who also worked at the airport as a red cap, said he heard about our band and wanted to hear us, to see if we were good enough for his club.

At first I didn't think I heard him right, so he said it again. He said if we were good enough he would pay us five dollars a man, a fish sandwich, and a bottle of soda. Without second-guessing him, I said yes. I was working the midnight shift, loading food onto the planes, and cleaning the dining room for the day shift. His comment about the band was like a breath of fresh air in a desert storm. Imagine! Getting paid for my piano playing!

Morgan's was the newest place in Kenner. Not the biggest, but the newest. We had never played anywhere and with Morgan's being new, that was hot. I couldn't wait to tell Leo the next morning, and I rushed home right after work. Normally I slept a few hours in the morning, but on this day I was too excited to sleep. I had to tell the band the news. We were going to get paid at Morgan's new club. Our first job! The band was as excited as I was.

I called us a band, but we really were a bunch of school friends. Leo was on drums, or what we called drums, and my cousin Clarence Butler was the real piano player. June Ivy, or Little Skeet, as we called him, was on guitar, Morris Burton on trumpet, and June Garden on sax. I was the singer. We thought we were the last word, and not one of us in the band was even seventeen.

When I finally calmed down from spreading the news it hit me, we only knew couple of songs: "Blue Moon" and one or two more. Mostly, we played those over and over. And most of the time I'd fake my piano playing. I had been to Morgan's one weekend to hear the band, and they played different songs all night long. What was I thinking? We couldn't do that. I was very disappointed and it nearly broke my heart, but I had to tell Mr. Morgan the truth. We weren't ready.

Disappointed, I knew what was needed, and I became more committed to the piano than ever. I tried my best to learn to play it really well, and my cousin, Clarence Johnson, suggested I take lessons, but to me that was the long way around. In two or three months we'd learned a lot more songs just by listening to records.

"Lloyd Price is not just a pioneer of rock 'n' roll, he just might well be the founding father."
—Offbeat Magazine

I had told Mr. Morgan that when we were ready, I'd be back. After weeks of rehearsals and me working at the piano, the time came when I felt we were ready, and we were! We played there for four or five Fridays, packing the house. Then my father found out, and when he did, all hell broke loose. To this day I don't know how he found out but as I was finishing a song on this particular Friday, I looked up and he was right there in front of me, on the stage, in my face. I was only sixteen.

"Git yor ass outta dis beer garden a 'fore I take dis good leg and crack yor shittin' ass," he shouted. "How dare you have yor li'l brother in here wit' all dis cussin', smokin', and drinkin' amongst dese grownups? He jus' fourteen year old."

My father, God rest his soul, took one of his crutches, hopped over me, knocked down the boxes and pans we used for drums, and broke up the show. Seeing my father do that was a real let down. He'd been my hero for so long, and the one who watched me struggle with that old piano trying my darndest to learn to play.

He was the one I had switched my life around to satisfy. He still couldn't work, and everything I did was to earn money to help him and the family. It seemed to me that he could've been a little more flexible and sensitive, more concerned about my feelings. That incident did not change how I felt about my dad, but it did make me realize how badly I wanted something for myself, something for me that no one could take away. I was more determined now than ever to play that piano. I think what I discovered then was that I had found my vision, and no matter what, I needed to stay focused.

It's true that I was hurt and embarrassed, but not enough to quit. I went on as if nothing had happened but there was a definite change in me. It was just like being chased by Ol' Jake, as it was a battle for my survival. I now had a "must do this" attitude. Soon after, we were back again, but this time we were stronger. My brother Leo had a full set of drums and everybody in the band seemed to boogie up with new instruments. There were a bunch of people who now wanted to play in the band. My dad was quiet about our efforts. He didn't encourage us to keep going, but he never tried to stop us again.

Morgan now paid us ten dollars a man, plus a soft drink of whatever kind of pop we wanted, and a sandwich. Looking back, when I really needed something to believe in, that was my positive proof that there is nothing like believing in yourself. I can't count the times we were laughed at by kids, and kids really know how to hurt each other, but all that embarrassment didn't phase me one bit. It was my dream. I was on a mission and driven by the belief that I could be in a band, that I could sing, and that I could play that piano.

3
Working at the Airport

While I worked at trying to balance music and school, Mr. Frankie, my boss at the restaurant, used to mess with me so much that one day I got to the point where I could no longer take it. I knew was going to quit if this guy stayed on me. One problem was that if there was nothing to do but make my life miserable, he'd just make up shit for me to do. There was no job description for any of us, just anything he thought of is what we did. If he saw us standing around in the kitchen doing nothing, you'd think it was a jailbreak from his excited alarm.

"Don't stand around doing nothing boy, find something to do. Ya' hear?"

I guess it was something about me he just didn't like. As for Kenner, it was a good job for a black kid my age, a four star restaurant in the airport, the Dobbs House, the best restaurant in town. On any given day anybody could be sitting in the dining room, from movie stars to the governor of the state. For our town, that was big, especially because all the upscale white people came to eat there before they flew away.

My mother's shop was not far from the airport. She had only fried fish and potato salad, but I helped her as much as I could, too. I liked my restaurant job, except for my boss. My plan was to quit and help her, but a cook at the Dobbs House, K.J. Jackson, had worked there much longer than I, and was much older and wiser.

"I need to remind you of something," he said. "Quitters don't win. So don't quit. Get even. If you quit, it'll always be on your mind. There's many ways to fight this cat. I used to be just like you when I first came here . . . mad, scared, and frustrated. I didn't want to get fired. Then I realized that I had the best hand.

"Think of it as a poker game with this honky. We cook his food. And every time he slaps or insults me, I play my hand. I put shit in his food, just go to the bathroom, get some pee, and put that in the soup pot. Then I sit back and watch him eat it. I laugh my ass off. I can poison that son-bitch whenever I want too. I can piss in the onion soup and he'll never know the difference. He'll think it's some kind of spice. I even chop roaches into his sweet rolls and put that wet, white sugar on 'em once they're baked. He never knows the difference.

"What I do to him depends on how he treats me," K.J. continued. "That son of a bitch has gotta eat and I'm his cook. I get even when I get mad with his ass. When he's okay and I'm not angry anymore, I smile and let him think I'm just another of his niggers. I don't know what he be thinking when he pisses me off and embarrasses me, talks to me like I'm nothing. I keep my head down and just go to the toilet and get my shit. You'd think after all this time they would've learned. Never kick a quiet snake."

Needless to say, what a great learning experience that turned out to be. Not that I ever put shit in anyone's food. I was not the cook, but I learned it's not how swift or fast or smart you think you are. That does not take you to the finish line first. K.J. showed me how to position myself to take advantage of my most valuable asset, my invisibleness of being black. I say invisible because white people act like they don't see black. We're just something they'd rather not deal with, and they continue to live in denial, as if there's no brain in our head.

My point is this: you can beat the guy who thinks he's unbeatable when he least suspects it. Do you think Mr. Frankie ever thought that K.J. put shit in the dark gravy, chopped roaches in the sweet rolls, and pee in the onion soup? No. To be sure, K.J. was not the smartest pot in the kitchen either, but Mr. Frankie never was the wiser. This all powerful earth beast, the one who knew everything, the ass kicker of little boys, thought he was a walking god with power over all. Let's see if he was smart enough to know when he was eating shit.

I don't think K.J. ever spent a single day in school, but to overcome the pain of insults, he used common sense, which most white folks thought black folks didn't have. K.J. didn't miss a beat whenever the boss complimented him on the food. "Food tastes like shit, K.J.," the boss would say. Then K.J. would do a little shuffle and dance and say, "Yassuh, boss," as if he was getting the golden spoon award for best cook. "Yassuh, boss. This sure is some good shit." K.J. always said that with a big wide grin. "I knows what you likes boss, and I fixed that stuffed pork chop with that good special spices gravy just the way you like it, boss."

Can you imagine? While that earth god was eating shit, K.J. was Uncle Tomin' it up and laughing. Yep. I learned a lot from that. Whenever Mr. Frankie put his foot in anyone's ass, K.J. put shit in his mouth, and he didn't have a clue. Mr. Frankie sarcastically thought he was the only one with a brain, and that his insults and abuses were invisible. I wonder if Ol' Jake had any black hands cooking his food, too. The mind is funny, how Ol' Jake and Mr. Frankie never recognized they were sumdumhonkys. It was no secret to us. We all knew.

What infuriated me more than anything was when I worked for a white man and he and his buddies often stood right next to me and told each other sick black jokes. This went on a lot in the South back then and jokes were always about a nigger.

"Hey Zack, did I ever tell you the one 'bout the nigga' and the white man playing 'Five Up'?

"No."

"The nigga' beat the white man, and was scared to pick it up."

Then they'd laugh 'til they were red in the face. I guessed the game Five Up was some kind of card game the white man and the nigger were playing. The nigger won but was scared to pick up his winnings. That was just one black joke they told, but they also talked about Jews, dagos, chinks, wetbacks, and punks. There was no limit to their jokes and no respect for my feelings. And, it was a continuous thing.

"I know you heard about 'the Jews,' ha, ha, ha."

"You don't catch the Jews?" another asked.

"What's the Jews, Joe, some kind of disease?"

"Yuk, yuk, yuk!" they'd all laugh. "You mean you don't know what a Jew is?

They're the ones moving into the white side of town who look just like niggers with white skin, green eyes, big fat lips, and a big nose. They kinda thinks they white, but Ol' Slim is fixing to give 'em a welcoming with a broke rib party."

They'd laugh again, and with me taking a page from K.J.'s book. I showed no fear and laughed right along with them as loud as I could. I had no idea what a "broke rib party" was, but by the time I finished laughing I'm sure they thought I knew all about that sick shit. It was not in the least bit funny.

Truth was, I didn't know what a Jew was either, and couldn't recall ever seeing one. Where I'm from nobody spoke of Jews. Either you were black, white, or a chink, period.

No, the south was not a cool place to be if you weren't white. Nothing you said or did would make them like you. What those people did was thought to be funny by them, but it wasn't funny when it was aimed at you. If you were a person of color, *you* were the joke.

While I was still a kid there was nothing I could do but bear it and grin. I may have crossed the state line once, into Mississippi or maybe Alabama. I didn't know much, but the whole world knew about Mississippi's white reputation and how they treated the blacks. Even though I had no choice but to accept the way things were, the treatment white people gave us was very difficult to bear and understand.

For those of you who are too young to know the old America, thank God for that blessing. This was not the greatest place to be not that long ago if you were black. If I live a thousand years I still could not explain the thinking of that white man. I mean this in no negative manner for many white people. It is just difficult for me to understand the way that kind of white man thought about me, a man of color, his full-blood cousin.

Most times a southern white man seemed to believe from the bottom of his heart that black people didn't deserve any respect or justice, and he gave you none. He could never think of a black man as a man, and what's so amazing, there's no way we could not be kin. Here in America today, it doesn't matter what he thinks. There are dozens of different shades of people of color in this country. Where did that come from and how did it happen? Hey, it didn't just happen. There had to be a mix of races to make the baby. If he wants to continue thinking we're invisible, that's another story. But the truth is right there in his face.

All this time's been wasted with the white man thinking we are going to go away and not be noticed. Why is that? Every one knows we are cousins. Did he really think separation would do the trick with two bathrooms, a black one and a white one? Blacks were not allowed to sit with him or eat at the same table and yet every night he looked for some black woman's bed to sleep in. Come on, Cuz, we didn't do it. You did. I gotta admit that it took a while, but you can come out of denial now. I must say your shit was smooth as silk for over four hundred years, but it's over now.

I used to hear my elders say that the only way to beat this kind of man was to find a new weapon that he couldn't beat you with. You can't out gun him, because the law is on his side. He *is* the law and don't try beating him up, because that would be suicide. You must show him something in you that he's never seen before. Look him in his eyes, no matter what he does to you, show him that there's courage in your soul. Let him feel what you feel: fear. Everyone feels fear. Let him see that you've gone as far as you can go, and that you have no intention of dying. Death is not for you alone, and the option is not just for the poor and helpless. Everyone dies.

Remember my father's saying, "if a rabbit could throw a rock there'd be less people hunting him in the bush?" That's something I'll always remember. I was not academically astute, so to survive and deal with the white SOB I needed to be creative in my thoughts. Courage was a new weapon for me and I started acting like a crazy man, even though I had no idea what would happen. Now, where I had always said "Yassuh," I said "No," and the difference began.

I started to see more respect and the pushing got a little softer, because everything they said to me now wasn't okay. You don't have to be violent to push back, just show some craziness at points where you feel vulnerable. In my day talking back was huge to somebody who was white, but you were immediately called a crazy nigger.

School never could've taught me how to not let insults humiliate me. The white man who thought he was God was good at making me feel that pain, but he would soon find out how ineffective his bullshit now was with me. Whenever he told sick jokes or called me a nigger, I'd just laugh. I might have even done a little jig, just to test his alertness. He was never on guard at anytime, and his confidence was such that he'd say anything to me or another black man. He trusted his soul to me at every level and felt secure in knowing there was nothing I could do about it. But now, now that was no longer so.

I used laughter as my defense. I didn't have a stick or a stone and don't think I would have used either. On hindsight I should have been more like the rabbit, just throw one rock, and these bigoted men might have stopped doing that shit around me, telling sick demeaning jokes. If I had just thrown one rock. But, I am not a violent man. Maybe they got the message anyway that I didn't think it was funny. Or maybe they realized there was a brain in my head after all. One day the jokes stopped and my fear of the people was gone.

4
My Piano

I won't take you back over my entire career, that would be difficult to do in one chapter. But to shorten it, I became a big teenage star in the early 1950s, perhaps the biggest that had ever been at that time. It was unheard of for a young black kid from the south to make the impact I made in the music world. In a nutshell, I hit the top, and my music revolutionized American teenagers and started the youth movement.

There was never a youth anything until "Lawdy Miss Clawdy," the first song I'd written. I wrote it while I was trying to learn how to play piano. Promoters and theater owners said the song had started something new, and most of them called it rock and roll.

In the beginning it was just another colored record, but I knew that "Lawdy" was high on the radio request list on all stations across the country, twenty-four hours a day. I could hear my voice on the radio, on both black and white stations, and the feeling was an experience far beyond anything I could've ever imagined. Who could ever have dreamed that blacks and whites would be dancing together and holding hands, laughing together while listening to music? At that time no one could've imagined it, but that's what happened. Music, my music, brought the two sides, the two races, together.

Today I see black and white kids, teens, and young adults sitting, together, working together, laughing together. These are the grandchildren of the youth of my day, and what a difference I see. Many of these youth don't see color; they just see people. I am so proud that started with music, and that "Lawdy Miss Clawdy" was a big part of it.

You know my feelings about my hometown and the white people who ran it. My only hope was to find a way out of Kenner. My belief was that if I got out and crossed the Mason Dixon line, I would no longer have a feeling of intimidation. With the success of my music, I was "somebody" now, and had the money to leave.

I can't explain the relief I felt after "Lawdy" hit, and I managed to travel a few places and saw that people really did treat me differently. But, home was home and I was still that boy who lived down the street. However, I wasn't that boy in my head anymore. Most people in my town were making forty-five, forty-six cents an hour. I was making three hundred fifty dollars a night, every night.

It was shocking to realize that I was making more money than the president of the United States. The feeling of being an underling was still there, though. For example, if I went into a store and didn't say "yes, 'em" or "yes, sir," the store clerk would quickly remind me with a "know your place, boy" look. Not that I minded. There were still those who didn't give hoot about decent treatment of blacks, but they were leaving my world fast. My parents were worried about me, so the best thing to do to keep my parents from worrying, was to find another place to live. It really was getting to be a bit much at their home in Kenner. Home had very quickly gotten too small.

Since such success was new to me, I wasn't sure how to handle it. For sure, this was like a rocket to the moon. Dates were being booked by several promoters and one white promoter, Eli Weinberg, who promoted black dances in many states, booked my first tour. My first big date was in Raleigh, North Carolina, and we then went on to Durham, which was just a stone's throw away. There was a big white college there in Durham. This was my first road trip east and I was looking forward to crossing that magic line where a black person was supposed to be free.

My agent's assistant, Ms. Evelyn Johnson, told me that whenever Mr. Weinberg brought a black artist into big white towns to work white dates, he didn't put the artist's picture on the posters. "Don't be surprised if you don't see your picture," she said. That struck me strange, since I was going across the line where black and white could mix. But, being my first time, I didn't know what to think. I was just excited to see what being free felt like.

Ms. Johnson did say however, that white college teenagers loved black radio and black music—and if they didn't actually see the face on the poster more than likely they would come to the dance. The students were from everywhere and with the school being so nearby, there would probably be a lot coming—especially with me playing the dance and making my first appearance. She was sure they would want to hear the new youth music live.

On the night I appeared in Raleigh there were three times as many whites in the audience as there were blacks. Nobody knew if it was a white dance or a black dance, and no one seemed concerned. Everything was going smoothly and I certainly was not expecting trouble. Then one white policeman saw the mixing of black and white dancing together, which he thought was wrong, and stopped the music.

All of a sudden all hell broke loose. Not in a violent way, but the crowd on the floor wanted to know why the band stopped playing. The place was crowded with several thousand people, but there had been no trouble. The policeman just would not accept the mixing. He had no other reason for the stoppage, so the kids got excited.

The promoter, Mr. Weinberg, didn't separate the colors. He just let everybody in. To tell the truth, I didn't know why the music had been stopped. It was only a dance and this one policeman was there for security. I had been starting to think I was finally done with all the race crap. I was across the Mason Dixon line, where I was supposed to be free.

What this policeman did, I couldn't believe it. He couldn't stand seeing black and white kids having a good time together so he came up with this genius idea of separating them. After he stopped the music, he put a rope down the middle of the dance floor, whites on one side and blacks on the other. There could be no mixing in North Carolina, he said. One side had to be considered as spectators, in order not to break the law.

First of all, I had never seen anything like this black and white dancing together on the same dance floor. I knew the kids were liking the music, but dancing together was a huge step up in my mind. A few minutes later, just outside my dressing room door, it was looking like a state police barracks. So many officers had come not understanding why they were there, as there was no trouble. I later learned the rope was not just to stop the mixing. The real reason for the rope was for something totally different.

But first, let me remind you, I was scared as hell. I was completely off target thinking I had crossed the line of safety and was free from the nigger-hating rednecks. It was more like jumping out of the pot into the fire. I must admit all my life I believed a white face was a white man, until I went to North Carolina and learned there was another racial twist to the hate that I didn't know about.

All white faces were not white men in North Carolina then. Eli Weinberg looked like any other white man to me, until I heard someone call him a smart-ass Jew. At first I didn't know what or who they were talking about, until one of them called his name. At that point I looked out my door and there were even more policemen. I didn't hear anything like a fight, and there was no white woman with me, so why were so many lawmen there?

The rope was up but it seemed like the town had had trouble before with Eli Weinberg. This night they were going to fix the problem, and what were they going to do? Hang him! I was having all kinds of thoughts when I heard one police officer say, "We got to stop that Jew from coming here with these damn dances. What's he's trying to do? He know we don't like no mixing in North Carolina. He's lucky we let him come here in da first place with his Jewish ass."

"Yeeeaah, buddy. We gotta stop him. A damn Jew is hard to be trusted," said another. "I'm gon' shine my shoes in his ass!"

They knew I was listening and talked all around me, even though the disrespect they had for Eli was the same feeling I felt they had for me. It couldn't have been any worse if they were talking directly to me. Then I thought about the many times white teens came to my dances and into my dressing room, but I always thought of them as spectators, because we never counted them as a paid part of the attendance for the percentage I received from nightly ticket sales.

The way a promoter like Weinberg worked was that he took all the money from the door and only paid the minimum guarantee, such as $350, to the performer. But in my contract, after a certain number of dollars over a certain amount, the artist and promoter split the overage fifty-fifty. Not only did Eli screw me, as his partner, out of the white attendance money, but he did the same to people in towns and cities wherever he could get away with it. Now, the police were there mainly to stop him from stealing from the club owner, as the owner also got a cut.

All of this happened more than sixty years ago, but the memory isn't dead. I won't let it die. In essence, the dividing rope did several things: it enabled organizers to count the white kids on one side of the rope, and also it separated them from the blacks. It also enabled the city and the club owner to catch Weinberg, and I got a fair count on the attendance.

You didn't have to be an Einstein to see what Weinberg was doing. Even if he paid me a lot of money, his commitment to be fair with the split of the fifty-fifty percentage was where he was dishonest. I knew I couldn't let this separate me from him, though, because I was new at this and it was something I needed to learn. I was always driven by new experiences and this was an opportunity of discovery.

That night I learned that the dream I'd had all my life, that certain parts of this country were different from the others, was wrong. I had never seen anything like it. A rope to separate was a true learning experience. I was out of Louisiana, so I thought I was free, but I learned it's not safe to close your eyes to the man on the horse. In church, in a police car, he could be your counselor or your doctor. Just be aware. Pay attention. If you're black, walk slow and laid back. He's watching you.

Today I have quite a number of Jewish friends. Some of them would not have given a shit, like in Raleigh, when the man put that rope down. But what the organizers did with that nonsense made me a little wiser. Yes, with each passing night I had not gotten my percentages from Eli Weinberg because I believed and trusted him. But these North Carolina people's hate for Jews put me on the right track, and taught me to be careful about who you trust. As far as being free, it was still just a dream.

We had never counted the white kids before then, meaning I was never paid for any white person in my audience. I had never received a percentage of their ticket price, as I did with black kids. I wasn't sure if they paid to come, but I was happy to see them liking my music the same as the black kids. When I heard the policeman talk in that tone of voice about Eli, about Mr. Weinberg, saying he was a crook, I realized that the word "crook" to me was the same as the grown men in white sheets. Crooked? Was that why they put that rope up?

According to Eli, white kids weren't supposed to be there, so he didn't charge them. He just let them in, and with that statement he double-crossed me and the venue and the city. Based on what the policeman said when he said, "Never trust a Jew," they were going to get him for back money. Did that mean he wasn't white when they called him a Jew? Because he wasn't a white redneck did it also mean he couldn't be trusted? And since he wasn't white, what was he? All these thoughts were running though my head.

One thing for sure, Hollywood movies led me to believe that when you became a big star you you could be free and the people who were your fans wanted to see you. That didn't mean anything in North Carolina. The white man's law was the only thing that mattered. Fair enough. Somewhere along the way I had forgotten my color.

Weinberg didn't seem to care about any color—or the law. He was only concerned with this new craze of white kids dancing to black music, and bending the rules a little to get them in as free spectators. But, he did not let them in free. That was money for his pocket.

My perspective at the time was different. I still wasn't free. It wasn't only the segregation, the gowned men, the redneck state troopers, and the Eli Weinberg's that stopped me from my freedom. There were so many other people and things I had to worry about. I was beginning to feel boxed in and could hardly carry all the responsibility and details in my head.

People also knew I was getting money, and they all had advice for me. Being a country boy who never had much of anything, I now had lawyers, accountants, promoters, agents, fans, band buses, cars, and payroll to deal with. I knew more about flying than I knew about all that, but my business affairs had to take precedence over looking for freedom. My responsibilities were not something I could walk away from. Needless to say, that was a lot for me, a country boy from Kenner, Louisiana. Until now, the most money I had ever seen at one time was twenty-six dollars and forty cents a week. What I needed now, more than anything, was help!

After realizing the world was not going to change just because I was making money, I went to the people I felt most comfortable with, my mother and father, and asked them for advice. What was more amazing to me than being chased by some redneck, they said they couldn't help me. I had forgotten that there hadn't been anyone in my family who was trained in anything except hard labor. They didn't want anything to do with what I was doing.

My father was not completely unsupportive, though. He had seen a white lawyer's picture in the paper, a man named Charles Levy, and suggested that I go see him. I did, and Mr. Levy said I would be his first black client. There was just one hook. He asked if I had five hundred dollars for a retainer. I had no idea what he meant by retainer. What was he talking about? What did the word mean?

Being one who asked a lot of questions, I did, and he told me it was an advance of money for the work he was going to do for me. I did look around to try to find a black man who could help me, since my experience was so limited with white people. All I knew was Ol' Jake and his boys. They had taught me to have little trust in white people. I knew there was no respect for me from the white man. I could tell by the way he looked at me and talked to me. Sometimes I could sense it in a voice. It was all hate, no passion. I still believed in Baptist and Christian teachings, and I believed there was good and bad in all of us. But I couldn't help asking myself why I had no trust for those people. Hate for them, however, never crossed my mind. I didn't know a Jew from a gentile, and wondered why I needed to know the difference.

Learning the business side of the music business was a bitch. There were no black attorneys in the business. In fact, there were hardly any blacks in anything. That's how Mr. Levy became my lawyer and it finally dawned on me that running my own business was not going to be anywhere near as easy as working in the kitchen at the Dobbs House. At first being on the road with my band was fun, but that enjoyment didn't last long. The fun was gone with the police thinking every car I drove I had stolen. And, any time I had light skinned woman with me, they thought I was a pimp. When they discovered she was black I'd be fined, just for the hell of it. Life was now full of business questions and answers, and I was supposed to know everything.

Then came a time to decide that Mr. Levy was not the right lawyer for me after all. I went to see a local black businessman that I knew, Mr. Rip Roberts. I told him what my problems were and that I needed help. He said the best he could do for me was wish me "good luck." I was looking for someone black, but there weren't any black lawyers that he could think of, not one single black man would be able to help me with my special situation.

Mr. Roberts said if I needed a certified public accountant (CPA) that there was only one licensed black CPA that he knew of in the country, and he was in Washington, DC. If I wanted someone to do basic stuff, such as bookkeeping, he could recommend a bookkeeper who might give me a start. This was 1952, when I really needed help. I was a new black kid in a business earning money and didn't know anything about the law or management. I knew nothing about government, but one of my business managers told me there were only seven hundred licensed black businessmen in America and over five hundred of them were morticians. I knew then that I was in trouble.

It was no secret that back in the early 1950s, just after WWII, that most of black America had never gone to college. That's why I found it very difficult to find a black CPA. It was like looking for a needle in a haystack and really drove it home for me. Here I was making all this money, a dumb, naïve, trusting kid who was trusting people who knew less than I did. My brother with his ninth grade education was my business manager. I needed help, had the money, but couldn't even buy it.

Why was it like that? I suppose the bell should've gone off in my head then about not just me, but how bad off my people were. I realized then there was a phrase that I would never use again. "Catch up" was the phrase we used whenever we referred to blacks as compared to white people. We could "catch up." From where I stood, all I had to do was look around to see that would never happen.

My brother Louis was doing my bookkeeping, he and my roadie's dad, Pops Mitchell. Neither was qualified, but at the time, how would I have known? I understood the concept of what was supposed to happen, but how to go about executing the idea of collecting the percentages every night was a big deal. None of us had ever seen or heard the word percentage. It was a first for all of us. I'm not saying we were stupid; I place it on not knowing.

You can't rush experience and I certainly had none of that. If there was an override of monies from the door of the fifty-fifty split between me and the promoter, instead of that money being counted as income to me they'd put it in their pocket as a personal tip, thinking it was something extra for doing a good job. This was instead of filling out the report of income for my records. I, of course, wasn't any the wiser. When my agent's assistant asked about my percentage and the night's report sheet, I'd tell her what my brother told me, and her answer was always, "What?"

I knew I had to do something about this; there was just no way I could run a business and be ignorant of the facts. In spite of all the love and glory I was getting as an artist, and the care I had for my brother, my soul had a hole in it because I couldn't do math well. My career opportunity came early, so I didn't get a chance to finish school. Money I had plenty of, but it was more than being uninformed that had me worried. I was beginning to discover the difficulty of being black and having to function in a white man's business world.

I had a lot of things going against me and one of the things that was truly uncomfortable was my southern accent and upbringing. In the rest of the country, that was a sure sign of ignorance. I had to stop the cheating in my business, and to stop being so Southern and country. I needed help with both of those things so Mr. Roberts suggested that I use a black man named Bill Boskent. He was in New York and able to talk like the big white businessmen. So I did, to save myself embarrassment. Talking and trying to do business throughout the country was very different from how it was in Kenner. I promised myself then that I would change.

5
Sudden Change

As we grow older we tend to let our minds review our souls, and sometimes we are amazed at ourselves—and the things our hearts have withstood. As I see it now, the white man of my younger days was a master sociologist—and a brutal one at that—because he knew how to downplay a black man's pride, not taking account of the fact that we had limited opportunities.

There was a time in America that a black dog had more rights, and was welcomed into more places, than a black man. A dog in the early fifties and sixties could walk through any front door and be welcome, whereas if a black man did the same thing he would've been arrested and sent to jail. There was hardly anything a black man could do that was not against the law.

What do you think that did to the black man's self esteem? He was beaten down as a man because somewhere in the recesses of his mind he saw a dog as being better than himself. You don't have to be a genius to know what that did to one's inner self, and I'm sure the white man was aware of it. He was the one who said what you see is what you believe.

Think of the pressure the colored man was under at all times. From the time he was brought to this continent against his will until a few decades ago many died believing they were nothing. And how about a black person not being able to walk on the grass of a white cemetery? That was illegal in most places in the south and it embarrasses me now just thinking about it.

As a kid, passing a white cemetery was like passing a white woman. I knew she was there but I was too scared to look at her because the repercussions could be devastating. If you were caught walking on the grass of a white cemetery in Kenner when I was a boy it was a sure way to get a slap on the head. Sometimes I used to wonder if any white person ever felt ashamed for the sociological pain they put us through. I imagine he thought the color of the skin was segregation, and that's where it stopped. But to a person of color, that was only the beginning.

The white man can't see the damage that humiliation causes inside your mind and body. To be insulted in that way, inside you became like a bottle of champagne corked up in the hot sun. A full-grown black man couldn't talk back to his white junior, or sit in a public place and have lunch, without being insulted. He had to beg to use the bathroom. Every door was closed to him, but it was okay for his dog! And yet he's told to believe in the word of their white Lord.

To believe in segregation, as we were told, and in the white man's bible, it meant that we had to accept the oppression that came with it. It's right smack in the center of their bible, the Lord Jesus Christ who looked exactly like him. It speaks volumes of who the bible favors, so how could it be a black man's salvation?

Why would the white man want to save us anyway, when all he ever tried to do was punish us? He has always been able to do whatever he liked, so if the white man represented God, our goose was cooked. Even though he was confused about us, none of us ever really believed the oppressor and the savior were one and the same.

In all truthfulness we probably believed more in the spiritual side of God than the white man did. Yet he continually tried to control us with fear and his boogieman mentality by feeding us bullshit about his heaven, his hell, his God, and his glory. There are many different kinds of religion in the white man's world, and I can't see in any of them that it's a black man's salvation. The most it was to us was an illusion, and in no way were we convinced.

Maybe we did trick the white man with the boogie woogie and the shuffle, making him think we believed while quietly keeping our own faith that there had to be a god somewhere out there who could save us. And He just might be a colored man. In all the black churches you could feel what they call spirit. You could see how people were affected by prayer. Every prayer had a reason, and those who prayed meant it from the heart and it came from the innocence of their soul. If they believed, there was something or someone who would come save them from all the pain, humiliation, and suffering that the white man caused. They believed it and knew it would not be the white man who'd come. Amazing how *he* didn't know that.

As I see it, who but children of God could take the kind of punishment black people have taken for all these years?

Who else could have the patience to put up with all of it without raising their voices or hands? To do that we had to believe in something greater, a more merciful power that protected us. How else could we have survived? The real believers know God exists.

I suppose in many ways hindsight is a good thing. For one, I'm now so very proud to be a black man. It's been rough, but I wouldn't trade my experiences for anything. How unique it is to be one of a kind. I used to hate my thick lips, kinky hair, and black skin, for no reason other than the perception others had of me.

But no man other than a black man can claim to be black and be recognized as easily as a bird in the sky. That's something I feel really good about, and am proud of. My ancestors had to have been very strong people. They even could be the lost tribe they spoke about in the white man's bible. Wouldn't that be a surprise!

What kind of blood is in our veins? Millions of us came from so few, I don't think any living creature has taken more abuse and survived as well as we have. Why have so many white men found something wrong with us, when we have nothing? I'm not saying we're the only ones who suffered, but why do they fear us? We are the ones in America who have given so much, and whose contributions still seem to be invisible.

6
He Hates Me for No Reason at All

I was drafted in 1953 and served in the US Army from Nov. 13, 1953 until October 20, 1955. Even though I was stationed in Korea after the official "end" of the Korean War, there was still fighting going on. There is still fighting going on in Korea today and some of our troops are still there, sixty years later.

Somewhere along the way in Korea I met a honky named Bubba. I believe he came from Missouri. I will never forget him, especially because he once told me that he couldn't think of anything lower than a nigger, and if he was not better than a nigger, what good was living anyway?

I never liked the arrogance of people like him. He was, to me, the king of sumdumhonky, and it's useless to say what I thought about him. I felt I was in Korea because I was illegally drafted. My music had pissed off some Dixie-crat senator and he thought the south was ready to rise again. He and his cronies said I had to go because I was causing young teenagers, black and white, to mix together, and integration was never going to happen on their watch, if God be their witness.

So, I was drafted and shipped overseas, and Bubba had a problem living in the same tent with niggers. As if I gave a shit about being there with him, after leaving my storybook life. His problem was new to him. He had never been around black folks and I had never lived with or seen how white people lived until I ended up in the army. Society was just going though integration and we were being forced to live together.

Bubba was pissed about our living arrangements until one night when Bed Check Charlie (the name we gave to enemy aircraft) crossed the thirty-eighth parallel and started to bomb everything in sight. That's when color didn't matter. If you were blue, Bubba wanted to be your friend. Either that or he wished he was a rat, so he could crawl in a hole and go underground.

The army trained us to dig our own foxholes for just such an emergency, and it was mandatory that each man knew where his hole was. On this particular winter night it was snowing so hard you could hardly see a foot in front of yourself. It was also so cold that if my rifle touched my skin it would have burned like fire, just as if I had sat on hot coals. I was hunkered down in my foxhole in all that mess when through the snow I saw Bubba running toward me.

"Let me in, let me in! I don't wanna die! Please let me in." Bubba was crying and screaming like a bitch and calling on his Lord.

As he tried to jump into my foxhole I stuck my bayonet in his face. "Hold up buddy," I said. "This is *my* foxhole. Can't you see the sign? It says 'for coloreds only.' Besides, tonight you don't have to run. These bombs tonight that Joe Chink is dropping are for the niggers, because we got no business being here anyway. Did you forget? *You* don't do nothing with niggers. *You* don't want niggers in your tent. So don't worry about Charlie. Those are nigger bombs tonight and they don't kill white people. Have you forgotten? Niggers and whites don't mix. They ain't supposed to die together, either. Ain't that against the law? Bed Check Charlie know we don't do anything together, not even die, you no-nuts motherfucker, and those are your words I'm using: niggers are lower than snakes. Remember? So get outta my foxhole!"

What fucking nerve he had, trying to get into my foxhole after telling me that he couldn't think of anything that was lower than a nigger. I was really tempted to let him wait, and let Joe Chink answer that question for him, to see whether niggers and whites can die together with a little napalm. That definitely would've shown that cracker, an idiot who couldn't get out of the way of his own shadow. He was a true redneck, a cowardly, snuff-dipping, certified nigger-hating fool who believed his ass was made of steel—until he saw danger. If you took nigger and Jesus Christ out of his vocabulary, this son-bitch would be speechless, and there he stood crying like a baby trying to get into my foxhole. What the hell was I supposed to do? Save him, the white man who I wish hadn't been born?

Yes. I did. I saved his ass. I let him in and believe me, I've been having trouble with that decision ever since. He was crying and begging like an Eighth Avenue whore who hadn't caught a trick all week and needed rent money, or she'd get busted by her pimp. It was a busy night and I went for it. There was a lot going on, and not knowing where Bed Check Charlie was, I really couldn't waste too much time with Bubba, so I let him in. It was a very cold night, so cold that I felt my teeth rattling. So, not knowing what was coming next, I compromised my principles. It wasn't that he got by me. Let's just say it was his lucky night and that *my* God was with him.

Bed Check Charlie didn't come our way that night. It blows my mind just thinking how sick Bubba was, that redneck honky really was a pickle. My wish would be for Bubba to feel what I felt when smothered by insults. And, there were millions more just like him. Once, just once, they should feel that humiliation. I still don't know how blacks made it this far without a real revolution. There was a period of civil rights in the sixties, and although it helped, it was nothing like a true revolution.

Everything a black man did to try and better himself for so many years, whatever it was, it was against white law. Not being able to pick the school of your choice for a decent education, it took a civil rights law to make that happen. Things are still a long way from acceptable, but it's better, and getting where the white man don't have so much control.

One thing still gets to me, and it's so painfully obvious. Look no farther than Washington. Prejudice there washes down the street like water down a mountain. You can feel it in a store waiting for service when there's no one but you. I see him, the store clerk who has just moved here from some other country. He sees me; it's just the two of us. He goes to the back for a minute and when he comes back there are now four of us: him, me and two white customers. He pretends he doesn't know who was next.

There must be a black god somewhere, because these fucking foreigners just got here. The ink on their green card is still wet, and they have learned to pretend they don't know who's next? It's not just the redneck whites, but the wanna be whites as well. And this one just got off the boat. He just looked right through me as if I weren't standing there.

Are black people really that invisible? How tall or fat is enough to be seen? How big does a black man have to be before he's respected? It seems that we are just one big afterthought to everybody. Even the foreigners. As soon as they get here they already know the drill of the redneck.

If you notice I use the word redneck a lot, it's the same as the white man uses the word nigger. I just want to be clear. What is so amazing is that black Americans have fought and died so foreigners who disrespect us can come here and eat bread on US soil.

I often talk about South Africa and apartheid, which is the way it used to be with blacks and whites here in America not that long ago. Being a second-class citizen and standing in the back of the line wasn't bad enough. For example, when a black person wanted to buy a hat, the deal was if he tried it on, he had to buy it. If it didn't fit, too bad, it was his.

Can you imagine standing in line to spend your hard earned money in a store, and not being able to piss in the same bowl with the honky? And the SOB who just stood beside you can't speak English. You fought for him to come here and he has more rights than you. What could be his reason for not liking you? I can understand the redneck, the home-grown white man, but a damn foreigner with an attitude, looking past me while I wait in his store for service longer than the white person who came in after me?

After all the years of fighting for equality in this country, blacks still went to war and died fighting in the defense of the flag and for the honor of our country. They worked for nearly nothing to help build roads and bridges to make America great, yet laws said if there was a line to stand in, niggers went to the back. Hundreds of years of suffering inhuman treatment, and foreigners who just arrived went to the front of the line in the banks and the business community while I can't get a "May I help you sir?" from this mother who works in the store.

I'll tell you something else. The American white man did one heck of a good job influencing others of the world with his hatred for us. He spread his word around the globe of how we should be treated. Is that anyway to treat a cousin?

Even the Japanese, with all their pain and suffering, had the nerve to give the black GI a lowlife nickname when I was there. They called him "chocolate ki'yum," which was a demeaning term for blacks. "Number hucking ten" was the same, a little stronger and, of course, meant blacks were the lowest thing on the totem pole. Naturally, number one was reserved for the white GI. He was "number hucking one."

7
I Don't Know How to Be a Racist

It would be honest to say that I did not feel the brunt of racism that most of my generation did because I was blessed with a recording contract early on. My love for music has been for as long as I can remember, and as a kid I followed bands wherever I could get in to hear them. I don't know if it was luck or being in the right place at the right time, or maybe it was because my mother had a sandwich shop with a piano and a juke box in it. I loved everything about music including that old piano.

Dave Bartholomew, a black bandleader in New Orleans, was the most popular band in town. He had been given the assignment to find young black singers to record for Specialty Records, a California outfit. This had never happened before, black teenagers being given the opportunity to make records.

One day Dave came into my mother's shop when I was picking away at a little song I had made up. I had been trying to learn how to play the chords on the piano that fit the song. It hadn't been easy for me to try to learn to play. I'd been working at it for a couple of years and was working as a part time piano player in our little band on weekends.

The song I had made up was called "Lawdy Miss Clawdy," but I didn't have a clue of knowing what an A-flat chord was, or any chord for that matter. But, that little song changed the sound of music forever. It was my start and my entire career developed from it. Traveling from city to city, playing clubs, I heard my music everywhere, and thousands of people came out to my concerts to see if I was real.

It was a moving experience, but it did not remove me from the one thing I dreaded the most. My success did not change the feelings and the minds of the white man. They still wanted me to sound and act like "I'm your nigger, yas-suh boss." Popularity didn't mean spit! Not all (I had won the respect of some), but at no time did the white man let me forget I was a nigger. I have to say I was good at it. Being from the south allowed me to deal with that better than most, as I'd had a lifetime of experience. I still don't understand what it is that makes us black people feel like we need to have acceptance of whites.

That's what gets me, when a white guy acts like he's happy to see me when I'm working, playing a show, or doing anything that makes money for him. He pretends we're best friends, but he never says, "Hey Lloyd, why don't you come spend the night at my house, and meet the folks while you're in town." Huh? I knew my place because they never let me forget it. I knew he could turn on me like the wind.

What he did say, when he wanted me to believe he was a friendly guy, was, "By the way Lloyd, did you boys find a place to stay? There're a few places 'cross town. I believe old fat Mary's place is the best colored house in this town." At least that's what I heard. It was always "cross town," or "over the tracks." He never said, "I checked you in right across the street in the hotel where I'm staying."

Even in the Northern states he didn't give a shit and thought I was too dumb to notice. Whenever a white man introduced me to one of his friends he introduced me title first, rather than name first. "Fred, you know that dance tonight? This is Lloyd Price. He's the one who made those records 'Personality,' 'Stagger Lee,' and 'Lawdy Miss Clawdy.'" No matter what I did, how much money I made, or how big I got, he never sat across the table and looked at me as an equal. There was always a way of letting "Fred" and his friends know I was a hired hand. One time in South Carolina a honky told me that he knew exactly how it felt for me to be a black man in the South, and that he'd probably feel the same way in New York City.

"'Stagger Lee' became a sensation when deejays discovered it on the flip side of 'You Need Love.' At one point it sold nearly 200,000 copies a day. 'Stagger Lee' rapidly shot to #1 on the pop charts."
—CBS.com

"If I was in New York," he said, "it would be mighty difficult to pretend everything was okay when I'd be crying on the inside knowing I was breaking every rule my parents taught me. I just wouldn't feel right sitting by a black man eating my dinner with him at the same table with me. My daddy told me, and his daddy before him, you just didn't do that. They said to not ever put a nigger at my level. It ain't right in the eyes of God. If it was God's intention for us to be together, he would've made us all the same color."

And all I'd asked him was if I could I use his restroom.

"Buddy," I said, "how could you ever know how I feel or what my level is? You don't know me from Adam. I'm spending my money with you, and you refuse to let me piss in your pressure toilet. My dick is certainly cleaner than my hands, and you're taking dirty black money from these black hands, then touching your face and scratching your chin. I didn't ask you if I could eat here, so you don't have the worry of a plate breaking. All I want is to take a piss in your shit house. And there's one more thing you should know. Don't tell ever tell a black man you know how he feels when your whole life experience has been built around what your daddy told you. The one thing he should have told you was to grow up."

No matter my words and feelings, the man simply shrugged his shoulders and said, "Well, you still can't use the restroom."

Being black in America means you have to try to survive, one more day, every day of your life. You are constantly being tried by a white, male, bald-headed jury and have little power. Most of these white men are just like their redneck daddies, with hundreds of years of hate in their bones. Daily in America, black men are tried for invisible crimes they never committed. The judge and jury are so old and outdated they could think Robert E. Lee is still president. These people already believe the black man is half monkey or even a "tree coon," so how could any trial be fair? What other judgment could there be for a tree coon, except guilty?

In the justice system, both state and federal, a black man's life is just one big game. In my opinion, the courts are for whites only. There was a time not so long ago when blacks were not allowed on the jury. In the eyes of the white man, blacks didn't warrant a fair trial of their peers, and if a white man pointed his finger and said the nigger was guilty, "innocent until proven guilty" did not apply. I don't care if it was New York, South Carolina, or California. Being tried was a joke.

Even now if I walk into a white restaurant where my black face is the only one they see, people stop eating and the room gets quiet—and it's not because they recognize me as a famous person. They're wondering what the hell am I doing there and when I am leaving. So sir, even if you live forever, don't ever tell me, a black man, that you know how I feel. That is an opportunity you will never have. You will never know what I feel.

I used to think it was a curse being black, and I wasn't the only black person to feel that way. Probably every black person in America wanted to be some other race at some point in his or her life. Can you imagine an entire race of people who are afraid that God didn't like black people?

Years ago if you asked a black American what his family bloodline was he would put everything in it, including the kitchen sink. He'd also say he wasn't quite sure where he came from, as his grandfather never wrote it down, or could not remember. But you could bet that his bloodline was from a white country like Ireland, Germany, France, or England. Of course, it could have been true, because America is a big melting pot, where everyone comes from somewhere. Nobody is from America, except the Indian, but if a man was as black as a tar baby he'd never—not ever—say his ancestors came from Africa. Didn't any of us ever look in the mirror?

What power fear has to make one deny his own heritage, image, origin, and homeland. But suppose, just suppose, it was the other way around. Suppose the great white honky had been smart enough to reach out and embrace blacks, treat us with dignity and humanity? Suppose he'd told us something about ourselves and not kept our history a secret from us, and let us speak in our own language and practice our own culture? Can you imagine what this country would be like? Many of the problems of today would not be.

Maybe with our brain mixed with his blood we could have made a real difference, had he allowed us to be free. But instead, he caged us with control and fear. Or, maybe it was he who had the real fear, knowing we were descendants of great kings and warriors, and had inventive minds that were capable of doing mighty things. Was it he, that mighty honky, who couldn't chance that someone might discover that we were human, too?

Suppose he had made it so we all worked together as one, back in the days of slavery, as we did more recently in rock and roll. Suppose we *all* had been "you for me and me for you." Imagine what the United States of America would mean to the world. We'd have no racial issues. Look at all the time that was wasted just to control the niggers. Look at what wealth was wasted when there shouldn't have been any cost at all if we were allowed to be free.

Instead, sumdumhonky thought caging the niggers was a good idea. Remember that we didn't ask to come here, and how long did you really think selling people like caged animals would last? After four hundred years of doing it, some of them still think it's a good idea, because in some areas of the world it is still going on. Don't take my word for it. Just take a look at the TV news. The reality is that black people today are more American than apple pie. I find it very sad that no one will ever know how much greater America could have been.

Since 1964 a few laws have been passed that said we were human after all and deserved certain civil rights. I don't believe that any of us would have had our moment in history, though, if it wasn't for the youth movement of black music. There was nothing more personal to one's heart and ears than a love of music.

When the white man finally started talking to us, it was because his sons and daughters had a love for our music. It was not Rosa Parks, or Martin Luther King, even though those were great people who did great things. The significant events they started means a lot in black history, but none of it could have happened if it wasn't already happening with our music.

There never could have been any uprising if there was no movement with the youth. When Rosa Parks sat on that bus in Alabama, the black music revolution was in full force with both black and white youth. They were already hooked. Something had to be in the wind for so many people of color to say "Hell no," to the drivers and the police. As bad as times were, the youth movement was already well on its way, and nothing was bringing the young people together like my music and the New Orleans sound. A new beginning had begun.

In 1953 I had been put in jail in Little Rock, Arkansas when I had gone there to play a dance. The police thought the Mexican girl who was with me was white, and someone spread the rumor that I had a white wife. The police stopped the dance that night and looked for mixing. Niggers couldn't have any woman that looked like a white woman, so they put me and the band in jail. Luckily, my driver had taken her out of town, so the police never did find her. In fact, they spent the whole night looking for her. Had they found her in my room, someone else would be telling you this story.

Everywhere I went it was the same, a near riot with white kids tearing the place up to see me, and black kids trying, too. The authorities hated this youth movement, and me, with a passion. I couldn't do anything about the success of my music, but the draft board told me in no uncertain terms they could stop it. The chairman of the United States Senate Committee on Armed Services in Washington, DC said I would be drafted, and I was.

"'Lawdy Miss Clawdy' is a rhythm & blues classic that helped give birth to rock and roll."
—Rock & Roll Hall of Fame

The powers that be felt they had to contain law and order in the South. By drafting me, my music would stop. So I was drafted, even though by law I wasn't supposed to go. Five of my brothers were already serving, but that made no difference. I was sent to Korea, but that didn't stop the interest kids had in black music. The youth movement was on and it was far too late for that.

The Civil Rights Act passed in 1964, more than ten years after I was jailed. The country was still at war with black music, but now the music had allies. A new generation of white boys and girls who had to have this music in their homes were now on the front lines. They were fighting for togetherness because they had been touched by the music and discovered we all have souls. They even tried to mimic it themselves.

I'm not saying that all these other things could not have happened, like the march on Washington for civil rights, which was very important. There surely were many people who suffered and died, which was such a travesty. For the first time, white kids became soldiers on behalf of the blacks. Even though we were descendents of great warriors, after hundreds of years of pain we never were successful at saving ourselves until the young white kids recognized our strength by loving black music. It became our weapon to fight with.

If not for segregation to control us, perhaps billions of dollars could've been saved for this country, and many advances made. It might have been my folks, black people, who had the cure for cancer by now, or discovered secret voices to communicate with aliens, found a way to travel deeper into space, or discovered a new universe. Who knows what might have happened had we been free.

To be so challenged, there must be something very special about us. Could it be the earth tones in our skin, or our perfect rhythm that put us in harmony with the universe? Or is it our spirit of peace that keeps us so well balanced that we are able to take on anything that comes our way and survive? Is that what keeps the white man so pissed off?

Think of it this way. Why are the rhythms of black music understood so clearly throughout the world? It is a genre of music that has crossed cultural and ethnic boundaries everywhere, and changed feelings toward one another. Wouldn't it have been better if we had communicated through music, rather than guns, and the only issues of black and white were notes that were played on a keyboard? Could our musical communication now with each other be the key to solving the problem of racism?

Our music started with the Africa drum, and won the hearts and souls of those who had felt, seen, and participated in dance halls across America. People had been abused by so many authorities, just so they could dance. It was a matter of time for American families when black met white, back-to-back on the dance floor. It was a time when they were in the streets together to right a wrong that had taken place for too long. In 1953, for the first time, when the guns from World War II and the Korean War went silent, the children of the confederacy and we blacks, together, we rejoiced.

Who is black, and who is white? I have cousins with red hair and green eyes, and their skins are as light as any other person who calls themselves white. My mother's father owned a ferryboat company and looking at his picture, I can't believe he was my grandfather, but should I call my mother a liar? He was as white as any white man I've seen. After all these years there's not much left that makes us African; our DNA has been so diluted by sumdumhonkys. It was some of his DNA that left the dance floors and took civil rights to the streets. And now, his white children know the truth about who we are.

My grandma had enough kids to make twenty-two different tones of blackness in their skin. And, my mother and her sister had twenty-two kids between them, eleven each in their families, all with different skin colors. In each family, we all had the same father. How do you suppose that happened? What is America if it isn't color, and how much more American can a person of color be?

After food and shelter, it's for certain that no spendable dollars were left in the poor Southern, black family's budget, because all they had for entertainment was sex. And to think that some sumdumhonky started all of it by raping his slave, our grandmamma. Our family growth is not going to slow down, that's here to stay, but in a sense it's good. He won't take responsibility for his own actions, and he screams denial on the highest mountaintop, but he will never live down our kinship. We're cousins, even though he made us to be controlled, but let me tell you a secret. If the earth survives a million more years he will never have the opportunity to dominate us again. We will not stand for it. We will not let it happen.

8
The Racist Car Dealers

Hollywood was not joking when it cast Buckwheat and Little Black Sambo as little picaninnies, and portrayed the three black crows in early movies as stupid, weak, and dumb. In its day, Hollywood was as big a racist promoter as any Southern senator. Hollywood was called the movie industry of the world, but they should have been called the agency for racism. It was, by far, the leader in sending segregated messages about blacks and destroying the character of black people. In the Hollywood system, even every cartoon they made fixed a negative image about black people in the mindsets of both black and white children.

At some point early in my career I was ready to buy a car—a nice one—and there was a Cadillac dealership at the corner of Sunset Boulevard near Specialty Records right there in Hollywood. But, the salesmen who saw me in their showroom must have taken me for Buckwheat. From their actions, these guys might have been members of the white knights, because my reception from them was the same as if

I had interrupted the burning of the cross in any town in Mississippi, where people of color weren't welcome.

I continued to look around, though, and saw a long, pretty, shiny white car on the showroom floor. Everything in me said I had to have it. Though I was a teenager who looked mature for his age, and I was emancipated, I was concerned about my age and the way I looked. However, I didn't anticipate any problems, as this was California. I waited for a salesman, but none of them took notice of me. I waited and waited, finally my impatience grew thin so I made a sign for one of the salesmen to come over, but I was ignored.

I don't know what I was thinking, other than I had to have that car, so I paid little attention to anything else. Finally I noticed that I was the only customer left in the showroom and no salesperson showed any interest in talking to me. After three times of trying to get their attention it hit me that these sons of bitches ain't coming over to see what I want. So, putting my best face on, I went to one of them. After all, this was Los Angeles, where all my cowboy heroes were. It was a place I doubted Ol' Jake had ever heard of. Surely I wasn't on his territory. Surely I wasn't going to encounter that same old bullshit of being black. It would not be a handicap here. It was very uncomfortable being black in Kenner, Louisiana, but this was Hollywood, California.

But, when I walked up to the salesman, he shocked me with his loud voice. "I been watchin' you boy," he said. "What the hell you want in here? And don't be wasting my time with nonsense! What is it you want here?"

Before I could tell him what I wanted he walked away, and disappeared through a door. I stood there, uncomfortable. I was so disappointed that even here, white people like this man suspected me as a troublemaker. Did he think I wanted to steal something? Before I could figure that out, another man came out, obviously to get rid of me.

"Lookahere, boy," he said. "You have seen enough. This ain't no picture show. What'ah, you want here anyway? Better still boy, hit the road."

I was frightened by this man's attitude, and he surely heard it in my voice. I reminded myself that he was just a redneck salesman. In fact, the two of them could have been extras who couldn't make it as actors, and were now selling cars.

"I . . . I ah, want to buy that car." I motioned to the white Cadillac.

The man broke out in a laugh so hard I thought he might hurt himself. "You wanna what? You wanna buy that car? Ha, ha, ha!" he said, pointing and laughing.

"Yes, sir."

"With *what*?"

"Money," I said.

"Do you have any idea what you're saying, boy?" Then he left me standing there and went back to his office, laughing all the way.

I stood there for a minute, watching the two men talk about me behind a glass window and laughing. I didn't like it one bit, being treated as if I was a joke. It was like Ol' Jake telling me to go back to Africa. Plus, I was afraid they'd call the police. I had done nothing but want to buy a car, but their suspicion of me did not feel right so I went out to a pay phone and called Art Rupe, the president of my record company, Specialty Records.

Art had just given me a big check and taken me to the bank to cash it. On the phone, I asked him to come and meet

"The first record I put out that seemed to catch the white market was 'Lawdy Miss Clawdy,'" said Specialty Records founder Art Rupe. "Back then, our records were only sold in the black part of town, so maybe the whites had somebody buy it for them. But after 'Lawdy Miss Clawdy,' white record stores were carrying our records. One copy of 'Lawdy Miss Clawdy' ended up in the hands of Elvis Presley, who recorded it for his first album."

me. Of course, when the salesmen saw Art, they came running with a big "May I help you, sir?" At the same time they looked at me along with Art, as if I was his shoe shine boy.

"You still here?" one of them said. "What'd I tell you boy?"

I had told Art what happened and the way the salesmen had treated me. By this time I was on my third or fourth hit record, and Art couldn't count all the money I was making for him. I could see that Art was disturbed by the attitude of the men at the dealership and knew it was a color thing.

"Which one of these cars you want, Lloyd?" Art asked.

I showed him.

Then Art said. "Which of these men didn't want to wait on you?"

"Neither of them actually," I said.

"Damn it! When is this stuff going to end?" Art mused, shaking his head. "A black man can't even buy a car without raising suspicion. This man," he said to the salesmen, "wants to buy that car. Is there something wrong with that?"

I wish I could describe the look on their faces. But in spite of how I was treated, I still had a soft spot and could only feel sorry for them in their big moment of embarrassment. I always wonder, though, why I can't ever recall any white man feeling sorry for me. I think about that a lot.

There were many reasons I shouldn't have bought that car. One for sure was the many insults the men hurled at me. But, I let that roll off my back, as there was no way for them to know I had four pockets full of hundred dollar bills. Plus, they had no idea I was the rage of this new youth movement in America. But in spite of all that, they could have asked me to leave in a nicer way, or they could even have taken me seriously as a customer before they eliminated me as a potential buyer of a new car.

Then I think, this happened in Hollywood, California in 1952, so please, tell me what is it about me that made me feel sorry for them?

9
On the Road in Mississippi

On my way home to Kenner, I wondered again why I bought the damn car, knowing that I had to drive a brand new Cadillac Fleetwood though the dark nights of Mississippi to get home to New Orleans. But to be truthful, it wasn't fun anywhere in the country if you were black and driving a Cadillac. I had a deep fear of the people of Mississippi, as their reputation was that if you were black, they'd have lunch while the dog bit you. They cared nothing about people of color at that time, and it was a place you didn't want to go if you were black, unless you had a death wish. It was that bad.

Sumdumhonky with a badge and gun in Mississippi would challenge you for your life, whether driving or walking. In that state they had no problem harassing you for being black. Plus, after all these years, I'm still shaken from an ordeal I went through in Biloxi, just after I bought the car from those Hollywood son-bitches.

Back then I knew the white man in Mississippi would sooner kill me than to tell me the time. I knew that, but I was also coming through their state in a new white Cadillac Fleetwood. To complicate matters, I had members of my band in the car with me. All of them were black, with slicked back, curly hair. To the bigoted, racist, white man, we were a car full of nigger pimps driving a brand new Cadillac that was stolen.

I could feel my heart coming though my chest. The last thing I wanted was to be stopped by one of these guys. You talk about sumdumhonkys. Mississippi was their birthplace.

It took a lot of faith and a white prayer to go through there as a black man, especially one as young as I was at the time. But, before I could finish my prayer, there was a honky cop behind me with his lights flashing.

I stopped, and from my rearview mirror watched as a big, six-foot fucker got out of his car and walked toward mine. Fear does dirty things to your mind, plays tricks with your emotions, and spins your heart like a time clock out of control, as it over-pumps fresh adrenalin. I sat there praying not to make a mistake when he talked to me.

Why was I so afraid of this man? Well, for one thing, even in the dark I could see that his uniform had that Nazi paratrooper look, grey with red and black stripes on the border of his sleeves. His boots were knee high and his pants looked like riding britches. He had a black leather strap across his chest that held his pistol and bullets, and just like every other honky I'd seen across America, he had a stone face. When he finally spoke there was nothing in his tone that implied that this was gonna be nice.

"Boy! Gimme yo lizence and yo registration an' make it pretty damn quick . . . gottdammitt hurr rup!" the state trooper demanded.

I had to think awful hard to understand what he was saying; his accent was that intense. I pulled out the requested papers and he examined them in such a way that I couldn't tell if he could read or not.

Then he said, "Did you see tha' damn speed limit thru here, boy?"

"Yassuh."

"Damn then. Why din't you obey it?"

"I wasn't going fast, sir."

"So I'm lyin', nigga'?"

"Oh, no, sir. No sir!"

"Git yor black ass outta tha' car, right now. Right Now! Git out *now*, and git over there." He pointed to a place on the shoulder of the road.

We were on Route 11 South, en route to New Orleans, and had to pass though Biloxi to get there. I had dreaded the fact that I had to go though here.

When I got out, he stuck his head into the car. "All you other niggas, git yo' asses outta tha' car, too. Come on, git out!" Then he asked, "Where's Mister Prize? Sumpin' ain't right here. Gimme yo' licenze! Dis here car got California registration and you niggers are here in Mississippi. Sumpin wrong here. Now. I'm gonna axe yo one more time. Where's Mister Lord Prize?"

"Sir, I—" He wouldn't let me finish.

"Nigga' jest answer me where he is."

"Sir, my name is Lloyd Price and this is my car, and these are members of my band."

"I know you ain't tellin' me this is *your* car, boy. This jus' ain't your car."

"Yassuh."

He put his hand on his gun. "Nigger, don't you play wit' me. I will blow your black head off."

"No *sir*, no, sir. I'm not playing with you, sir. I know better than that. Sir, this *is* my car. I'm that 'Lawdy Miss Clawdy' man. I make records, sir. Everybody who likes music knows me, sir. I will never play with you. No sir. Never."

"What you mean your dat 'Lawdy Miss Clawdy' man?"

That's a song I made, sir. Everybody likes it everywhere, sir. I don't know bout Mississippi, but they like it everywhere else, sir. I'm a musician, sir. I play piano."

"Now let's get this straight. Ya say this is your car and you're a musician and ya play music and makes records and that record makes 'nuff money to by this car? Is that what yer tellin' me, boy?"

"Yassuh." I had a feeling I might be getting through to him.

He scratched his head, thought for a minute then said, "Then all y'all clam your asses back in there. We goin' to see the judge. Boy, I been on the police force twenty-seven years, twenty-seven, an' I can't 'ford no car like this an' you goin' to tell me that's yours? Uh huh. Start 'er up. We goin' to the judge."

Here we were in a white Cadillac at two or three o'clock in the morning on a Mississippi highway following a mad, redneck trooper. It couldn't get any worse. If I had to compare my fear to anything, it would have been like in the nineteen thirties and forties when Adolph Hitler's storm troopers came in the middle of the night, and took the Jewish people on a ride to nowhere.

All of us were scared. We had no idea where this honky was taking us, but I'm sure we all had Bull Connor in mind.

Bull Connor was the commissioner of public safety for Birmingham, Alabama and was later head of the Alabama Public Service Commission. When he was in Birmingham, he oversaw the Birmingham fire and police departments, and was the man who directed those fire hoses and police attack dogs against demonstrators, including the children of protestors. Because Connor tried to enforce segregation and deny civil rights to blacks, he became an international symbol of racism, and we blacks feared him.

Bull Connor was the law then, and I still can't go to Mississippi without thinking about him. He was the one who said if a nigger voted for him he would not accept the vote. I also think about Emmett Till, even though this was just before that happened. Emmett was a black teenager who was murdered in 1956 in Mississippi, after speaking with a white woman. Emmett was fourteen.

I've known no fear like driving through Mississippi at night. I didn't know what I was going to do if we were going to see Bull Connor. As it pertained to the blacks in Mississippi, he was the meanest white man in the state—and you had to go some to get that honor. You have to wonder, how did he sleep at night? My experience had been that it was real hard for me to find in my mind a nice white man in the south who would give me an honest smile or an even chance. You just never knew why he was laughing when he looked at you.

As we drove to see the judge, it was a real bright night with a high moon and I hoped like hell that the trooper was taking us to that place Ol' Jake always talked about, Africa. I really wished for that. In fact, I wanted to go anywhere but to the woods in Mississippi. For the first time in my life I was having good feelings about Ol' Jake. That boat back to Africa was really making sense now.

We ended up going to a house on the outskirts of Biloxi. You know, that suburban kind of house with the white picket fence, two dogs in the yard, and a noose hanging in the basement. I was right behind the trooper when he pulled into the yard. He got out and pointed at me.

"You come with me. The rest y'all stay put."

Believe it or not, at that point all my fear left me. Every bit. *Ain't no way I'm going out like this*, I thought to myself. I didn't know what I was going to do, but I did know that fear was not the answer. *If it's just him and the judge, regardless of how big that sucker is, I ain't going down like that*, I thought.

Trust me, your mind plays trick with your common sense. I weighed one hundred and sixty pounds.

The door was unlocked and we went into the house. The trooper turned on the light and I felt a lot better when I saw it was a room set up like a courtroom. Well, it had a big chair behind a big desk for the judge to sit.

"Have a seat, Prize, 'til the judge come out."

"Yassuh."

"So boy, ya say ya play music?'

"Yassuh."

"I used to play music myself. Was a drummer up there in Chi-cargo. Thought I had left Mississippi for good, but I'm back again."

"What happened, sir? Why are you back, sir?" I was only pretending to be interested.

He paused for several moments. While he thought he looked straight at me. When he spoke, for the first time I was able to understand every word he said. "Well, Prize, I jest couldn't take it. First of all, I don't believe God 'tended for black people and white people to be together, huggin' and kissin' and all that. I jest don't believe in that, and that's why I left Chi-cargo. I worked in a club and ever' night this nigger came with his trashy white woman. She be rubbin' him on his black head and kissin' on his neck. I jest couldn't take it. Nosir, buddy. I couldn't take it. I know I'll never see that here in Mississippi so I came back home an' got on the police force. Down here, Prize, we do what God intended. If'n He wanted blacks and whites together, He would a made us all one color. All blacks, or all whites. Is that right Prize?"

"Yassuh, *yes sir*! One color, yassuh. We would all be one color."

"Damn. I jest can't understand what the hell a white woman sees in a damn nigger. He's jest a nigger."

You damn dumhonky. I didn't say that, but I sure was thinking it.

Just then the judge came in looking pissed off because he'd just gotten out of bed. He was a little bitty man who wore a tattered Confederate flag robe.

"Stand up, Prize," said the trooper.

I jumped up and damn near saluted that son-bitch.

"What we got here, Scooter?" the red-eyed judge asked.

"Well, Judge, this car came into our city limit driving a little wild. He was criss-crossing tha line, goin' back an' forth, so I pulled him over an' figured I'd have a talk with the driver. To my surprise when I got to the window of the car and looked in, it was a bunch of em' in there. Judge, I made this one git out first, then all of 'em. He was drivin' this high priced car . . . a Cadillac. Hardly ever seen one of them 'round here. This boy says the car's his. He's some kinda musician, says he made a record name of 'Lawdy Mister Clawdy.' Anyway, Judge, I been talkin' to him and I think we ought let this one go."

The judge scratched his bald head. "If that's how you feel Scooter, then this case is dismissed, and Scooter, dammit, don't wake me up no more tonight."

Damn if I wasn't confused. Suppose the judge had told Scooter to shoot me? Outside, the trooper told me why he let me go. "Prize, I let you go because there's somethin' 'bout you made me do it. I jest can't put my finger on it. But I really do believe that you believe what we believe."

It was pure bullshit if he believed that I believed what he believed, but this honky had a lot of confidence in himself when it came to black people. Here's an ass telling me to put the rope around my neck and jump off the box. It won't hurt, 'cause he said it wouldn't. That's the confidence they had trusting the nigger, thinking he would do anything they said. But, I found I was getting really good at dancing and shuffling around all this white crap.

10
You Don't Know Me

In any history, there are many little people of greatness who go unnoticed. Not that African history is small, but why is it that a black man's skin has to be associated with oppression before it is important enough to be written about?

What about Crispus Attucks who gave his life in 1770 in Boston for a noble cause in America? He was the first casualty in the Revolutionary War. Benjamin Banneker, a free African astronomer and mathematician, was hired by Thomas Jefferson in 1790 to help survey the District of Columbia. And, he gave America its first almanac.

Phillis Wheatley was sold as a slave at the age of eight to John Wheatley of Boston. She wrote poems and was the first African American woman to have a book of poems published. Then there was Simon of Cyrene. He was an African who was compelled by the Romans to carry the cross of Jesus when Jesus was taken to his crucifixion.

Why are these things not taught in our black schools or history books? Rodney King, a construction worker who was beaten by Los Angeles police officers following a high-speed car chase in 1991 was bigger news than the man who helped carry the cross of Jesus. More than two thousand years later, the story of Simon of Cyrene is still potent. Shouldn't that be taught somewhere, when the subject of Jesus comes up, that Simon was there?

The keepers of history have a way of not always favoring the real heroes, because a lot of them are just plain folks. In historical writings I've learned a lot about them, the people of color who, according to the writers of history, had no history.

Before 1952, if a black man found a way to penetrate the white world of entertainment, it wasn't because he got any help from the white press. It was because his talent was so extraordinary, word got around on its own and whites with privilege would come to see them in black clubs. Black entertainers were so good back then they might've presented a threat to the big people like Bing Crosby, Bob Hope, and the like, so the press didn't say a word about black entertainers unless it was negative.

It's true that Duke Ellington and Cab Calloway had something special—other than being half white. They didn't sing you know, not like real singers, they were bandleaders and posed no threat of getting off that bandstand to dance with a white woman. Cab did do some chanting and dancing, but for the most part those two just stayed on the stage and grinned.

Oh, the press gave them a line or two in the newspaper if they hung out with a white woman in Joe's after hours club in Paris, or were seen holding a white woman's hand in Georgia. But for anything else, you had to be a Louis (Satchmo)

Armstrong to get a mention in a white magazine or newspaper.

I'm not saying that Satch, who was a great trumpet player, wasn't deserving of what he got, but there was also Billy Eckstine, who at one time was more popular than Swiss cheese, and got nowhere near the publicity Satchmo got. Billy was a singer and bandleader of the swing era and his press was biggest when he was seen kissing a white woman in Hollywood. To put it another way, Billy Eckstine was as big as Frank Sinatra in the eyes of all the ladies, black or white. At one point in his career he was as big as Elvis.

Singer Nat King Cole had to switch from a musical trio to a solo artist when he began to work with Nelson Riddle of the Nelson Riddle Orchestra. Nat didn't have Mr. B's good looks (Billy Eckstine was sometimes called Mr. B.) but prior to Mr. B., whenever a black entertainer got mentioned, it was negative.

In the early 1950s, even though my music changed the way Americans listened to music, I got no press. Three years after I hit, there was a kid named Elvis Presley from Tupelo, Mississippi. The press was so excited; it seemed like they had discovered something that would cure cancer. In reality, they were excited about something that had already been done in many forms.

It was no secret that they didn't want niggers to own that music. Elvis just shook his leg and that was good enough. The only difference between the press Elvis and I got was race. He even kind of sounded like us. That wasn't Elvis's fault, but you couldn't keep the press away. I hold nothing but good in my heart for Elvis Presley, but these white guys who head the press will eventually meet their maker. I'm just making a point about how biased the American press was, and is.

Look what they did to Paul Robeson when he became a big star in the hit play *Othello*. In 1943 he became the first black actor to lead a Broadway play with a white supporting cast. The singer /actor also became involved as an activist for civil rights causes and the movement to advance people of color. For his efforts, he was branded as a communist and run out of the country. Robeson was such a great talent. Women of all colors loved him, but because of his beliefs of freedom and a free society, he felt he had to leave.

When I was drafted I absolutely did not want to be in Korea, but the strategy of the government was to silence my music, and stop the kids from integrating on the dance floor in the south. Maybe they were hoping I'd catch a bullet.

In spite of being mad at the world for being in Korea, and not realizing at first what was happening on the political front, I got a chance to witness first hand that some promises made by an American president came true. In the worst of times the president did what he said he would do. All of my life up to that point, and being a second-class citizen, it seemed like it was natural for presidents to lie when it came to us, but President Dwight D. Eisenhower kept the promise President Harry S. Truman made when he said there would be no more segregation in the army. At that point there was no law that said I couldn't piss in the same toilet bowl as the whites, or sit at the same table to eat, but hearts of all hearts the true redneck didn't like it. Most of my fellow soldiers thought niggers should work in the kitchen peeling potatoes and washing dishes, or cleaning the bathrooms.

What was so amazing was that we were all there representing the same flag, and carrying the same guns to kill the same enemy, and Bubba and his friends had a problem with niggers sleeping in the same tent with them. I must say, though, that for the first time in my life I felt we were all just American, and the hell with what they thought.

In addition to sleeping in the same room with white soldiers and sharing my foxhole with one or two of them, I also entertained the troops. Still, I was just another Bo Jangles. It was very clear that segregation didn't turn on and off like a light switch. I had to be aware of the Bubbas of the world, as they didn't give up that easy. Many still harbored a feeling of being betrayed by God and country, even if a black man was giving them enjoyment through his music.

That was then and this is now. To some extent to this day if a black man is in the music business, if he isn't wearing lipstick or a wig and earrings, or something else to put a dent his image as a man, there's only a slim chance that he'll get proper coverage from the press. There's got to be something wrong with him, or he has to have four or five felonies to boost the writer's ego. Otherwise there will be no story.

The black artist can't only have pure talent, because the press will hardly write about that, or his achievements. There would have to be some "freaky deaky" shit somewhere, something they found to write about, and for the life of me I can't figure out what being freaky has to do with talent.

I have spent my life trying to figure out what exactly rock and roll is. Historically speaking, before I recorded "Lawdy Miss Clawdy" in 1952, all black music was "race music." I had never heard black music being called anything else but that, but those are the same chords used to play rock and roll music. They are the same chords in "Lawdy" and other songs like it.

Why take something black people created and rename it? If you don't like it when we do it, no matter what you name it, it's still black music. You can't change the structure of the chords with a name. They are all the same. The drumbeat went a little crazy, but the chords those white boys in the 1950s were using were the same as we what we used when playing the blues. So how did it become rock and roll?

White folks just have to have a title for black folks talent. If he was a great jazz singer, he was labeled "Scatman, the blues singer," as John Paul Larkin (Scatman John) was called. Great black dancers were called "Fast Foot Willies," or "Lighting," as with Sam John Hopkins (Lightnin' Hopkins). A good musician, even a classical one, was called a "beebopper."

Marian Anderson, the great contralto opera star, was considered a good "race singer." In 1939, the Daughters of the American Revolution (DAR) refused to allow Anderson to sing to an integrated audience in Constitution Hall in Washington, DC. The refusal placed Anderson into the spotlight of the international community. With the aid of First Lady Eleanor Roosevelt and her husband, President Franklin D. Roosevelt, Anderson performed an open-air concert on Easter Sunday, April 9, 1939, on the steps of the Lincoln Memorial. She sang before a crowd of over seventy-five thousand people and a radio audience in the millions.

Her career might have been over had it been left up to prejudiced people who made a stink about her singing in such an important place as Constitution Hall. Those people, who I'm ashamed to call cousin, would have deprived so many of her wonderful voice. And Marian herself might have died without ever knowing how much she was appreciated.

Rhythm is the foundation of all those art forms I'm speaking of, and if a black performer didn't have it, no matter what he was called, it didn't count. You could not do anything without that rhythm. It is buried so deep in our so-called race music.

Later, I figured out why the name was changed from "race music" to rock and roll. It was to fit an accepted title, one that wouldn't offend those who didn't like nigger music, but loved rock and roll. Their teenage kids loved to dance to that youth music. Because you had to have rhythm, and that couldn't be copied, they just called it "bubble gum" or "swing." I wish more people knew that, in itself, has its roots in race music.

11
Savior

"Oldie but Goodie." Maybe all the name changing was done to undermine the real creators, the makers of race music, because both the music and the performer would have less value with such a degrading brand. The white man of my youth was really good at devaluing anything with color, a strong lesson learned from Willie Lynch. That honky, in a speech delivered on the banks of the James River in the Virginia colony in 1712, said about the making of a slave, "If you mark 'em it'll last a thousand years."

Just as it was then, it is now. We are reliving Lynch's vision. With the Oldie but Goodie title affecting songwriters and performers, it affects one's mental negotiating strength by being placed in such a weak category. The reason for the title change was to control, as it's always been when it comes to people of color. Strip a man of his mental strength, and it doesn't take much else to rob a few dollars from his music.

Illiteracy and necessity created short visions for artists, and more trust in their lawyers. In most cases, the lawyers screwed them. Look how big the music business has gotten, and who has gotten the most? The lawyers.

If the creators of race music had kept their ground and owned it, there would be no Oldie but Goodie shows now. The artists and songwriters would be in the same the league as The Beatles, The Rolling Stones, The Beach Boys, Elton John, Frank Sinatra, even Irving Berlin, or any of the other big white groups whose music didn't get renamed and still has mass appeal and earns millions. Why aren't they called Oldie but Goodie when all their music is well over fifty years old?

I'd guess that somewhere around 80 percent of all the music you hear today on TV or radio is some form of race music of the fifties and sixties. Yet, black music is called oldie after ten years or less, and the hole was dug even deeper when they started calling it "Old School." Out of sheer ignorance the black DJ of today thinks by saying Old School, it is something smart, hip, or cool. But, what he's really doing is killing the artist, and taking food off the table of his household.

You never hear the term Old School on white radio because it's a negative, and a negative is never cool. It's the same as saying an old person has no more use. Your wife, for instance, she would be an oldie but goodie. That term gets buried in the heart, mind, and souls of the black listener. Then again, there is a problem about the arts, and the artists who think it's a hip or cool term to say, especially when he hears his name on TV. These entertainers don't have a clue about the damage that's being done to their product, and neither does the listener. What's so amazing about all of this is only the black people think that big negative is cool.

I wonder why Cole Porter and other writers of his era aren't called Oldie but Goodie. There was a lot good about that music when it came out, and all of those artists predate the fifties and sixties by several decades. Did you know that some of the greatest commercial music in the world was written during the fifties and sixties by black artists?

You never hear a radio station anywhere say, "Here's an oldie by Elvis Presley." The man's been dead longer than the Rock & Roll Hall of Fame has been open. But, if the world didn't know he was dead, from the radio play he still gets and the marketing and promotion of his name, you'd think he was just around the corner doing a movie.

You never hear anything about Otis Blackwell, the black demo singer and writer who sang on almost every hit Elvis had. Elvis copied Otis when he recorded. There's nothing wrong with that. I'm just telling it straight. Not once have I ever heard or seen where anyone said anything about Otis or his children.

This makes no sense. While the families of the creators of the music, the artists and songwriters, can't find burial money for their dead husbands and fathers, here come little companies who call themselves royalty lenders. These companies somehow have inside knowledge, and know the conditions of these families. They wait around like flying vultures over their loved ones graves, knowing the heirs don't have a clue. These companies know that most of the children of artists and songwriters are brainless when it comes to the business of music. Then they wave a loan check like bait in the water.

The family, of course, steps into the pit. Not knowing that the show is a business, these bandits take advantage of them. They lie and cheat the families out of their rightfully earned income and rights to the music. These bastards are more than manipulators; they're the monster in these families' worst nightmare. What they do is a crime, and something should be done about it. To be fair, this happens to the families of songwriters of every color.

The way I see it this Oldie but Goodie thing, the title was designed to pay artists and songwriters less, and to make one think the work had no value. It was a genius of an idea, a perfect vehicle to steal. It affected our self-esteem in the same way it did when we were sent to the back door for a cup of coffee or a sandwich, and with that mindset it was like shooting fish in a bucket. Is it any wonder that we were set up to be taken by anyone with pink skin? It is as clear to me as a deer in my headlights.

The system also had us believing that the sonofabitch who offered those crappy loans were our saviors. Yes, they came after some artists and songwriters even before we all kicked the bucket. We took it as a favor. But, by giving us a small percentage of our own material and charging 50 percent on the few dollars the company loaned us (with compound interest each month) the loan without any question was the way they planned to take everything we had.

They really screwed us songwriters, and they knew it. They took advantage of our innocence by giving us a tiny slice of our own pie, and they ate the rest. Plus, they stole the pie pan. All of them should be arrested. If they're dead, I hope somebody wakes 'em up and puts their asses in jail.

Don't be fooled by that Old School, Oldie but Goodie bullshit. It's all business, and it's a trap. It's all figure, figure, figure, all for the white man, and nothing for the nigger.

Something in me always knew something was wrong with that picture, but when I started out we were all just kids with a dream. We trusted them with our hearts and they stole our trust, and our money.

In the beginning it was just us, the black artists and songwriters that showed up with the song. In this case it was rhythm and blues music. No whites would come near it or put it on their airwaves to be played. Like in any kid's life, you trust, so with a cup of coffee and a nice speech that felt like respect, we all thought we had a friend in a stranger. No, it wasn't just the press we didn't get, we get didn't justice or fair play from those royalty assholes who we trusted.

In 1952, I was at the heart and soul of this new beat from New Orleans. They say I was the first black teenage idol and Shirley Temple was the white one. I don't think anyone knew what to make of it. I certainly didn't. At seventeen, when I started writing songs, I had no idea of stardom. I didn't know what it meant when they said I was hotter than a piece of glass in the desert and somebody needed to pour ice water on me to cool me down, or I would burn up. What did all that mean?

I was told there never had been anyone like me or my music. They said I was a big star. I wondered why people wanted to touch me, to see if I was real, as they sang my songs. It was an amazing experience.

That was a fun time, but I didn't take it too seriously. I honestly didn't, but the white town folks took it very seriously. They'd fought all their lives to keep their sons and daughters from mixing with the common Negro. It was something they preached with a passion all their lives. Stay away from that colored man.

It probably never entered these white parents' minds that their innocent young children would want to dance and be sociable with young innocent colored kids—without a hint of racism. That went beneath everything the Southern white parent stood for, and I don't think they quite understood what it was that made their kids jump up and down like monkeys, as they said about the colored people. What was it that made them wanna act like niggers?

I for one certainly didn't know, but unbeknownst to me, I had found a way to connect with both black and white youth alike. I didn't know what I was doing, but my music had taken hold and made it happen. And, while it was happening, I don't think the white man could believe his eyes when he saw his children mixing with us. For him it must have been like watching his children being hung, or caught in a burning fire, which might have been more acceptable to him. Anything was probably better than having his children forget tradition and their upbringing, and all the prejudice and hate they had harbored all their life and handed down to their children.

So what happened? Back in the day you were supposed to believe "if you ain't white you ain't right." That meant hating every person who wasn't white. So why did these children wanted to mix with the coloreds? In all their outrageous devilment, the one thing white parents overlooked was that their kids had a human spirit, and were not the barbaric, primitive, unsophisticated animals they were.

Even the kids didn't even know what had happened to them. When they felt the power and the magic of a song, the beat slipped up on them and got inside their heads, just like the emotion of love. They didn't see it coming. They didn't feel black or white with music. No one does. All you feel is the power of the song and you love the music the same way you fell in love on a blind date. You can try, but you can't tell your heart who and when to love. That's a feeling that is far stronger than hate, and it's uncontrollable.

From the second those kids fell in love with the music, it had them and there was nothing they could do about it. For them it was love at first sound and they were hooked. It had to have broken the white man's heart to recognize the great power in nigger music. His children had been reared to obey his rules, so this was creating serious trouble in his family. Where I lived, black and white children did what daddy said, with no questions asked, but that was before the big beat came. And with the beat came new problems, new words to learn, and one word in particular that no one in my generation had ever heard before: integration.

Soon after that, music surfaced with a rock beat in it. White politicians began to flood the radio stations saying things like, "This town will never integrate!" "There's no power on earth that'll make me let a nigger dance with my daughters! I will burn in hell first." What was that all about? I seriously doubt if anyone knew what they were talking about, because who had ever heard of integration? Until the white man drew that line in the sand and made so much fuss about it, we didn't have a clue. Not until he brought that word to the table.

For a small child, or even a teenager, understanding adults is not an easy thing and I was no exception. It was difficult for me to understand old, bald-headed white men, and as far as white people in general, I didn't understand them at all. But, I think I do now. I used to wonder what could they be thinking. What harm could come from dancing that made them so upset, especially when everyone seemed to get such fun and enjoyment from it. Have you ever seen anybody dancing who is mad? I see people dancing all the time and I never saw anybody on the dance floor who was pissed off. Not ever.

"Lloyd Price's 'Stagger Lee' sold more than a million copies and was the top R&B record of 1959." –IMDB.com

When "Lawdy Miss Clawdy" hit the streets with the drum beat of an African rhythm played with sticks instead of the bare hands, that intoxicating rhythm in itself was revolutionary. So was our singing in broken and very bad English. What were they afraid of? Did they think their children had gone crazy because they had gotten a hold of it and loved it? Did the white man know then that the beat was as addictive as drugs, and no matter where people heard it, it made them happy? What was the fear, because people had to hear the song again, and again? Even now I can't sit still whenever I hear it.

Nothing was wrong with any of that until sumdumhonky saw a nigger "slooowww dancing" with his daughter. How does that grab ya? She had her hands wrapped around his neck and he hugged her around her waist, and she liked it. That's when the white man knew he had a problem. Boy, I bet that was something! Can you imagine what the white man felt? It had to leave him senseless about his daughter. She enjoyed being hugged by a colored man! The only question left was how to stop this runaway train.

I must admit that it took some time, but I saw what the white man had coming. All the sociological, mental, abusive, and cruel treatment he'd caused us for hundreds of years was nothing like what was ahead for him. If he lived forever with the habitual violence and injustice he'd caused us, it would be nothing compared to what was in store. And, there was nothing he could do to stop it.

Why did he have such fear? Grandchildren! Little half-white niggers running through his house with shit in their pants, snot and boogers hanging out of their noses calling him grandpa, his daughter wearing dread locks, the nigger boyfriend lying on the couch with a half-lit joint watching TV, scratching his nuts. Then the doorbell rings. He peeps through the peep hole to see who it was its and, surprise, its Ol' Jake with his new hood for the cross burning to-night. In this rage of excitement the white man runs through the room wondering, Lord what if Ol' Jake sees this?

Integration was something he fought against for so long that he treated it like a terminal disease. He even passed laws against white people being in the same room with blacks. One law in Alabama made it illegal in restaurants to have whites and blacks in the same room, unless they were separated by a seven-foot or higher wall. And, death to the nigger that looked into the eyes of a white lady. Pick up any newspaper in the red states from the 1930s though the seventies. The white man wasn't ashamed about how he felt. He wanted the world to know his feelings, but he definitely didn't want any of his friends to know what was going on in his house.

This shit was all that he started, and whatever it took he knew he had to stop it. The beat had given colored folks a lot of freedom, because they were now coming into his home not as workers, but as invited and welcomed guests of his own children. This new youth music was played on his hi-fi system.

The choice was his. If he put the music out he would lose the respect of his children. Or, the music could stay. He knew we were there, and we were there to stay. It had to have driven him crazy. He knew his children were the future. He loved them, but they had heard the call of the drums and life was never, ever going to be the same.

12
If it Wasn't for Big Mamma

I often wonder how smart and strong our people really were with all the hardship we've been through. When you think about it, it's a wonder any of us are still here. I'm sure if it was left up to him, this earth god, we'd all be dead and served up as dog food. So, there must be a god that serves us that the white man hasn't discovered. Otherwise he would have found a way to kill that god, too.

One thing the white man found in blackness and tried to keep all for himself was Big Mamma. He loved her and lusted after her, and I am willing to bet a dollar to a dime that's what saved us. Forget about being stolen from your tribe, your family in Africa and stored in the bottom of an old beat up wooden ship for months at a time, surviving on scraps and sweet potatoes whenever they were thrown at you in the hole. Forget about living with and surviving every disease known to man with no medical or doctor care. All of that was nothing. Just thank God, whoever God is, for the blessing of Big Mamma. She knew how to save us. She showed that white man her big, black fat ass and he went crazy. He couldn't resist that voluptuously sensual, sexually attractive woman, and that's what saved us. The only reason we're here today is that Big Mamma knew the power of sex.

Can you imagine? The first time he decided he was going to try a black woman? It was survival time, and I can assure you that when Big Mamma laid it on him he'd never seen nothing like it. He didn't know what hit him. After, he took her into the house. That's when his wife essentially became a slave, too. Her freedom was as limited as the niggers in the yard, as she was not allowed to even look at them. He also knew what he had found in Big Mamma, and didn't want his wife to find that same joy in Old Sam.

You may wonder why there are so many different shades of us colored people and why we call sumdumhonky a MF. Well, he earned the name. We are his children. How else could it be when he forced Grandmamma to lay them big fat lips on him? He thought he had died and gone home to see his Lord. He really got hooked, and that's the reason for all the different colors of colored folks. Sex! He couldn't get enough of it, and he's still going after it after all these years. It's the American DNA, black and white.

It's an undeniable truth that sex saved us, otherwise there would be no us. Now he hates us for it, because he became addicted to black and all the thanks goes to Big Mamma. Let me tell you something about the power of a black woman. It's love power. You've not been kissed until you've been kissed by a black woman. Thank you, Grandmamma. We are the rainbow, and it's all owed to you.

Did you know our daddy's are still loving black women? So many tricks are white men with black prostitutes. You hardly ever see or hear of a nigger getting busted for buying pussy, but the white segregationist just can't live without that black. I guess it's in his blood. Even though we are of his blood, he's the first son-bitch to deny it.

Segregation now, tomorrow, and forever. It's the biggest scam in the white man's history. What he really wanted was Big Mamma. Segregation was the cover up for him to keep Big Mamma. He wanted her for himself. He wanted to bring her into the house. And he never wanted his little lily-white wife to know he was doing the black maid. He didn't buy sex. He wanted to own it and would find an excuse to hang the maid's husband or boyfriend. That would justify his keeping her in the house as a live-in, because she now had nowhere to go. How awful that he used segregation for the cover up when he killed her man. Segregation was also the joke he played on his wife when he pretended to hate niggers.

"Honey, you tell me if a nigger just looks at you. I'll fix that black SOB. I'll kill him," he'd say. And he did. Many of us died because of his love for our black women.

Poor nigger didn't do shit other than being the maid's boyfriend or husband. The pity of the white man is that he stuck his chest out as a big man in the white neighborhood for hanging a nigger. Do you think he knew how small he really was? He should've asked his wife. If he thought she didn't know he was screwing the maid, was that sumdumhonky or what?

Years ago it was common to have more nannies in the kitchen with the boss's babies than there was cotton in the fields. Those of us with just a teeny, tiny brain knew that. Actually, something had to be wrong with the white man's mind if he thought we didn't know that. Most of all, what did he think a black man's daughter would say when her daddy asked who was the father of her baby? "It's hissun, Mr. John's, that's the baby's daddy." So her daddy would go and see Mr. John. Do I need to tell you what's next? Daddy never came home again and this sucker, Mr. John, went on drinking with the boys. To him it was just another dead nigger and a sunny day in Florida.

Another common occurrence was that the black nanny had complete run of the household, as well as the kitchen. The wife had little to say about anything. She had no voice. In a sense, the wife was under the same control as the black man, and can you guess why? It was because the black woman was sleeping with her husband. The only time the wife got any attention at all is when she lied about a black man. She'd tell her husband the nigger winked at her, and he'd have the nigger killed to show his love for his wife. In the mean time he's got Sadie back there in the kitchen. Hundreds of black men were hung for allegedly eyeing white women, while the white woman was as much in slavery as the black man. She wasn't even allowed to have eye-to-eye contact with him.

What puzzles me is that we blacks have been here almost as long as the whites and they pretend they don't know shit about us. Everybody can't be stupid, so why is he pretending? We've slept in his house, cooked his food, fed his family, chopped his wood, picked his cotton, made covers for his bed, and put clothes on his back. When he was sick we made the tonic that made him well. We even took his jackasses and plowed his fields so he could eat.

He then repays us by sexing our women, using them as his private stock, making a bunch of babies, and leaving us as bird shit by passing us in public like we don't exist. But here's the hook. What he knows least about us is what he fears the most. He thinks white women want black men. That might be true in some cases, but black men love their black women better than pork chops, so his biggest worry about his cousins should have been his least.

The only shameful thing he didn't see, or want to see, that shamed and embarrassed him, was that every time he hung a man of color it was one of his cousins. Sometimes it was his half brother and he thinks we don't know. Sumdumhonky.

▲

It's dawning on me that by now you might be thinking I'm a racist, but truly, I'm not. It irks me to no end when I hear it said that a black man is a racist. How can that be? What I do know is that it's not that complicated. Whatever I am and who I am, my honky cousins taught me. As a child I had nothing and knew nothing. He was the one who branded me, so I was what the honky said I was. Don't make me a racist, that's your problem.

The food my fathers ate, you gave to him. We also learned from you. Whatever societal manners we have or don't have came from you. All the books we read, you wrote, and you even designed the prayers we were taught to pray.

For hundreds of years you, my honky cousin, told blacks what they were and who they were. Yes, it was you who taught me racism with separation, which I now think was a good thing. Good in a sense that without we blacks having one another, I think you would have won. There'd be no us.

However, I don't think I'm a racist in the sense that you are. None of my friends think so either—and most of them are white. For the most part, I don't think segregation turned out to be what sumdumhonky intended it to be, but for us, it was the ties that bind. It kept the struggle together, and as we say, kept hope alive.

Even after all that I'm still not yet called an American. I call myself one, but my white honky cousins don't. They'd much rather give me another brand. I'm known as an African American. Other blacks might feel differently, but I'd just like to be considered American.

How easy is it to dismiss me, and others like me, as I sit and watch people from all over the world hold their hands up and make a pledge of citizenship to America. After a few years of them being here and becoming "American," all I get to be is partially American. African American.

In the last soon to be five hundred years between blacks and whites we have fought wars together and died together for the privilege of freedom on our godforsaken ground. With all that you call me a racist? I'm not. I don't know how to be one, and really, it's a joke when someone white calls a black man a racist. That is your game. You made the rules, and remember, I am only what you made me.

If it also sounds like I don't like white people, that's not true either. But if I don't like some of them, it's because they see me as something I am not. Ever since "Lawdy Miss Clawdy," I have lived in a white world. Actually, it's been lily white. I personally don't have a race problem and most everything I do has been with white people. In fact, I was around them so much I damn near thought I was white, not as an American, but as a white person. If you think I was racist in the sense like sumdumhonky is, no I never had that thought.

I have wanted and tried all my life to be what I know I am, a true black American. I am a veteran of the United States Army, not the Black Army of the United States. I don't know how to be anything else, but no matter what, at every station of my life I'm reminded that I am the other, even though I have embraced my citizenship.

I've served my country with pride, paid my share of taxes, and for more than a half a century employed many more who paid taxes. It's never been a question of my love for my country, but no matter how much I love her, she won't love me back.

When I was a kid everybody who I thought was somebody was white, so I can't dislike people just because of that. In a sense, I became one of them and because I was a poor boy from the country that had reached higher ground, there was no way I wanted to go back. I wanted to stay in the way of life that had been drilled into my head as the good life. I enjoyed the wine, the women, and the song, and this was sometimes resented by my white cousins. They can make a person feel real low with their demeaning nicknames. But I know who I am, so I refuse to accept that crap. I don't let it bother me. We blacks ain't going back.

To know what it's like being a "somebody" you must know what it's like being a "nobody." That's when it becomes very clear. I never was going to be the boy I was in Kenner after being a soldier in Korea and listening to the Honorable Elijah Mohammad. After that I realized I should always have been allowed to be an American, and made to believe that I was welcome. If that had happened I might not have felt as bad or as guilty about my color. Maybe I wouldn't have inherited any bad feelings. It was the white man who shamed me of who and what I am. So no, I won't go back to the little boy I was in Kenner.

13
Step-by-Step

As an entertainer, in traveling you get to see a lot of things and you learn from it. I used to work sometimes for a black promoter in Texas, a man named Howard Lewis. He booked a lot of dates on me. I point out his race because in those days in many small towns and hamlets the term "big nigger" meant something. All the little niggers had respect for the big nigger because he was the white man's nigger and had his blessing.

By the time I met Howard he was so big in his territory he covered all of Texas. Whenever I went there I figured I'd make a lot of money with him. Work was endless and he was one big promoter. On one trip, on my way to Texas for Howard, I stopped in Savannah, Georgia. I saw a new car dealership so I was treating myself to a new car.

I hadn't long gotten out of the army and my new song "Just Because" was burning up the radio. It was a smash hit and my old car, the one I'd gotten in Hollywood, had a lot of miles. With my new hit record I could well afford a new car.

The dealership was right on the main highway going though Savannah. It was a Cadillac dealership and my new car was right there in the window. It was a monster of a car, a pink and white drop top convertible. I had to have it. I just had to! It was almost the same feeling I had when I got my other new car, back in California.

Unconsciously, however, I guess I still had a bad attitude with white people, especially after dealing with guys like that Missouri cracker, Bubba, in Korea, who believed in nothing but Jesus Christ and segregation. Here I was a grown man with a name. I was one of the best-known names in the country then, but to get a sandwich I couldn't walk though the front door. No. I had to go around to the back of a restaurant.

The reason I bring that up is because here I was getting ready to spend thousands of dollars for a car and as soon as I walked in the door I saw the bathroom signs on the doors: ladies, gentlemen, and colored. Two years of my life had just been wasted ducking bullets and eating dog meat trying to save the damn Koreans. Now back here in my country, the only place I know as home, I had to put up with this? At the time I thought, if I'm only recognized as a full American when I die, don't bring the damn flag to my grave. In fact, you know what? You can take that moment of citizenship and stick it. Death is death, and the only requirement for that is dirt. With those kinds of memories, as badly as I wanted that car, I almost turned around and walked out.

America: In God We Trust? In the 1950s this was the land of the white man and if you weren't a member of the club, you didn't count. With this thought in my head I bought the car, but everything in me kept saying *don't do it.* In the beginning it was going smooth. A nigger dealing with a white man in Georgia had always been a problem, and now there was this salesman who was "too nice to be true." This just can't be, I thought, but believe it or not, I was almost out the door before the shit hit the fan.

This was back in the day when car insurance was not mandatory. You just picked up your car, changed tags, and you were on your way. Even with what happened on that Mississippi highway with that crazy state trooper and my other car, I had never paid attention to any of that registration crap. The salesman here seemed a bit too nice to be a white man, so how could I trust anything he said?

When I took the tags off my old car and put them on the new one, finally he had something to say. He saw a problem with that, as he thought my tags had expired.

Right away I jumped the gun. "Bullshit!" I said. The word just flew out of my mouth. "Are you blind?" I asked. "Can't you see nineteen fifty-six and fifty-seven on these tags? This is fifty-seven."

I lived in Washington, DC then, and the tags had a two-year life span, no matter what time of year you bought the car. I was mad and just that quick I felt blood rush to my head. The nerve of this honky, thinking niggers don't know shit.

"Sir," he said, "you just bought a car from me and I'm not going to argue with you. I just have to write on the papers what I see."

"It's really not an argument," I said. "I live in DC. You live in Georgia, so how can there be an argument? You're telling me about a DC tag? What's that got to do with me driving my car to Texas?"

Mind you, I have to admit I was still a little cocky, and still mad at the world and the army for taking me away from a life I was building for myself and my family. I was still mad at Bubba and Korea, and in this salesman I saw Bubba and every other redneck I had ever met. Maybe I overreacted because I was deep in redneck territory, but to tell the truth, I didn't give a hoot. You couldn't get much deeper in the south than Savannah, Georgia, unless it was Kenner, Louisiana. With the heavy chip I was carrying on my shoulder, though, I knew I had to be careful.

At times I wished I was Joe Louis, the boxing great, so I could physically express what I felt. Besides, I didn't want a Georgia tag on my car anyway. At times in New York I often went to Harlem to hear the brothers speak at the Rockland Palace on West 158th. This was something new to me. Brothers met brothers, and with a Georgia tag, surely I would have gotten my top cut and tires sliced.

The late 1950s was the worst time in my life because it was a horrible time to be black in America. Not that it's a great deal better now. Watch Fox News or any of the other major cable stations. It's certainly not news that is fair and balanced. But, the fifties was the beginning of the integration period and the earth god was on edge. Finally, it seemed there was a weakness in his heaven.

Little black kids wanted to go to better schools so they burned down the old ones. They could be better Americans with better schools, and what an uproar that was in the white kingdom. You would've thought the black devil was coming, but justice had taken off the blindfold. Not for some, but for all, and the white man turned loose their dogs and water cannons on the future seeds of this country. Babies carrying books were washed down the pavement like discarded trash, all just to show the rest of world how tough the white man was on their niggers.

But, you can't stop a wild plant root from growing. Many tried to kill it, it died a thousand times, but it will still grow. What the white man showed the world during this time was that he was sumdumhonky. With all that hate, the late fifties began to bring about a changing of times. It felt like all the black people on earth heard the call at the same time. Even throughout Africa and beyond, the call was "Hell No! We're not going to take it anymore!"

We all heard the bell. I had seen it coming with my first record in the dance halls. But, being young, my eyes saw things that my brain could not comprehend or communicate to me to pay attention. But now, here was something I was paying attention to, and I couldn't wait to see how it would all turn out.

Something else I was waiting to see was the end of the two contracts I had signed a few years before. I had signed these two contracts blindly, under the umbrella of my mother and father's parenthood, even though my lawyer, Mr. Levy, had spoken to them about taking me to be emancipated when I was eighteen. In 1952 I didn't have the first idea what that meant, or what a contract meant. As a child then, you were under your parents guidance until you were twenty-one, so they signed for me. I knew they had no idea what they had signed either. How could they have known without ever seeing a recording contract before? At any rate, I was told after I was emancipated that I was able to do anything except vote. All I wanted was my contracts back, first to try and understand them, then go into business for myself.

I was still amazed that I got a recording contract at all. Before I was signed to Specialty Records I had never heard the word contract—not in school or anywhere else, and why should I? There was never a need for any such document in our house, and nobody I knew ever mentioned one. A lawyer? There was never a need for one. Nor did I know that a lawyer should advise me. When I realized that signing a contract was a serious component of doing business, I had to do something about it and the first thing I wanted to do was get the first one I had signed, back. I had since learned that my terms were not very good, so for my own self-preservation I needed to find the strength to get out of those contracts.

I called Art Rupe, the president of Specialty Records, and told him I was unhappy and wanted a release. He first went through all of the surprise motions, as if he had just discovered he was pregnant. Then he said he'd call me back in a day or so to let me know. And he did. He said he had thought about it and it would cost me one thousand dollars for the release.

"You're charging me one thousand dollars for something I gave you for free?" I asked. I had trusted him with my life, plus it was I who turned him on to his newest star, Richard Penniman, a kid you might have heard of by now called Little Richard. While I was in the army overseas I'd gotten a letter from my mother saying that Mr. Rupe wanted to get in touch with me. I was on tour in Japan where there only were phones at the USO or the PX club for the soldiers on R&R (rest and recuperation).

I found a phone and called Mr. Rupe, and one thing led to another. During our conversation he said I'd be washed up before I was twenty-one. I didn't have any songs in the can to be put out, so in other words, I was finished. In the heat of his insults, which included me being dumb and stupid, I told him about this singer who jumped onto my stage in Georgia, banging away on the piano. His name was Little Richard.

"Is he anything like you?" Mr. Rupe asked.

"I think so," I said. "People seem to like him."

"How can I find him?"

I told Mr. Rupe to ask my brother, Leo, and the rest, as you know, is history. Bob Marley shot the sheriff, and by me giving Little Richard a break at Specialty, it was over for me. I shot myself in the foot when Art Rupe found Richard, and by the time I got out of the army Richard had taken my spot at Specialty Records. That was fine, he was a real talent and every loss is some gain.

I was happy that it was Little Richard who took my place. The only downer was when Mr. Rupe charged me one thousand dollars for my release. The reason for the charge, he said, was that he'd made me a commodity and I now had value. I didn't think that was fair. After all, Richard was selling records like a gold rush. But, I paid Mr. Rupe.

I went through a similar scenario with my other contract, the one with Don Roby at the Buffalo Booking Agency. I asked Ms. Johnson at that office for a release, and she went through the same motions.

"Aren't we good enough for you?" she asked. "Those New Yorkers must have gotten to you."

It wasn't anything like that. I just wanted a clean start, but in the end it was the same as Rupe. She wanted a thousand dollars for the release. It seemed to me like they had been talking, as they reached the same conclusion. What was

The Wagon Wheel Club in Dallas, Texas in 1952. L-R: Bill Jones, Lawrence Mario, Nellie Sims, Charles Otis, and me.

On stage at The Creole Palace in San Diego, California in 1952. L-R: Hugh Louis, Lawrence Mario, Bo Collins, me, Jack Wallas, and Charles Otis.

Left: I was just eighteen when I made my first trip to Hollywood, California. I was so excited to see the stars!

Right: My dad and me in 1953 in Hollywood, California at the *Cash Box* Awards. Dad is holding the award for my first gold record, "Lawdy Miss Clawdy," in his hand.

At the *Cash Box* Awards show in 1953. The man on the left and the woman in the middle were either with the City of Los Angeles or the awards. My dad is on the right.

Right: I am proud of my service to my country. The writing on the photo says: *With Love to Mom and Dad, Lloyd.*

Below: A promo picture taken in 1960 in New York City. Didn't I have some cool hair?

Below: With Jay Black ("Cara Mia," "Come a Little Bit Closer," and "This Magic Moment") on tour with Dick Clark's Caravan of the Stars in 1961.

My brother Leo on drums at The Celebrity Club in Amityville, Long Island in 1960 or 1961.

In 1968 at a club I owned in New York City on Broadway, The Turntable.

In 1970, just a few years before I left for Africa, this photo was taken outside my apartment in Philadelphia, Pennsylvania.

In my New York City office in the late 1970s writing a song between trips to Africa.

My brothers and me. L-R; Charles, Elbridge, Lloyd, Herman, Julius, and Louis Jr. My brother Leo is missing from this shot.

I later moved to Nigeria and was involved with a big boxing match and concert with Don King called Rumble in the Jungle. Here I am with H. Rap Brown, a friend of the family, Muhammad Ali, and my nephew, Lloyd.

Despite my initial experience, I ended up living in Africa for many years, and came to embrace the culture there. In the end, though, I came home to America.

You gotta love the tux in this 1980s era promo photo!

In 1994 I got to guest on a television show in New Orleans. At one time I thought I'd never go back to Southern Louisiana, but more recently the people have been kinder.

In May of 2001 I was honored by Southern University in New Orleans, Louisiana with a Doctor of Letters degree.

Above in 2007 at the Resort Hotel in Atlantic City, New Jersey, and (right) in 2014 on the Malt Shop Cruise (photo by Dollie Simpson). I have never stopped loving to sing or perform.

so amazing, little did I know, but my contracts with both of them were long finished. They stole my money from me, and took advantage of me. How else would each of them want a thousand dollars for a contract that had already expired? They knew I didn't know, and had me believe my time in the service was dead time, and that by law I had to extend the term of the contract to make up that lost time.

"Lloyd Price helped launch the careers of other artists, including Little Richard, who says, 'He is the reason, the cause of my recording career. I met him and told him I had a tape that I wanted him to listen to. Lloyd discovered me.'"
—People Magazine

Unfortunately for me, I bought their bullshit. There were, in some cases, time extensions with big government contracts, but not with my entertainment contracts. I later realized that they used me in a way that taught me something: people really do know when you're stupid. I promised myself from that time on that I would know what to say when I spoke, where to say it and who to say it to when I did. I'd also know how to count when I needed to, and those are promises I have never broken.

14
My Need to Know

At age twenty-one I opened my first office at 913 U Street NW in Washington, DC. The office was for my first record company and my first publishing company, companies that were all my own! Dell-Co was my publishing company and KRC (Kent Recording Company, or Kent Records), was my record label. At the time it was very adventurous for an artist to have a record label. Few, if any, artists had ever tried that before, black or white, but I didn't see it as a big deal. The only thing that could have been complicated was distribution and a hit would've taken care of that, because if you had a hit the distributor would find you.

I knew that, but the label was just the first part of the plan for why I had the office. The real purpose was for learning. My learning. I wanted to learn how to do business and what better place for that than Washington, DC? Bill Boskent was still with me as my business tutor. He had been with me as my tutor before I was drafted into the army, and I had a lot of trust in him and the other people I called the office boys, Billy Stewart and Don Covay. Both were great writers.

I didn't know them when I first opened my office. Being a brand new business I hardly knew anybody. I was just back from Korea and Billy and Don told me they were singers and songwriters. Being a record company, at that time the only one in Washington, DC, it was natural for writers and singers to come by. Usually, they wanted to be recorded or have their songs heard, but I wasn't interested in recording anybody or listening. There were other things on my mind at that time, like getting my ship sailing again.

To be honest I didn't know why I had Billy and Don there. Back then all record companies had what were called music rooms, but I didn't have the first clue how that was connected to publishing. Music rooms, I later came to find, were where writers spent the day to write songs. I didn't know it then, but that's what the music business was: songwriters and songwriting. In that respect, they were way ahead of me. The music business was founded on good writers, and here I had two of the best, and who later became world famous.

Don even received a pioneer award from the Rhythm and Blues Foundation in 1994. You might know him as the writer of Aretha Franklin's hit, "Chain of Fools." Billy was an amazing scat singer and was inducted posthumously into the Washington Area Music Association Hall of Fame in 2002. I didn't recognize their talent when they were in my office daily, but remember, I gave Little Richard to Art Rupe.

I eventually took Bill Boskent in as a partner. He was the guy Mr. Rip Roberts said I should use as a bookkeeper to "catch up" when I was looking for a black accountant. Bill was neither black nor white. He was known as a "high yellow Louisiana Cajun Negro." He was well-educated, smart, and an ex-pentagon officer. I really depended on him to teach me what I needed to know, and my expectations were high.

In addition to learning about business in general, I was interested in learning math, how to count, do high numbers correctly, and other business in this new world of music. But, it turned out that neither of us really knew anything about the record business or record labels. I was thinking this was a smart guy, smart enough to do anything. And, thinking because he was half white, my appeal would always be to his black side. No, he didn't know anything about the music business but I trusted him enough to get it right. You may not know this, but back in 1956 *all* business was new to black businessmen.

I can't help myself that whenever I need to say something important, I throw in the white thing. I guess over the years I can tell a brother the truth about something and he'll question it, but if a white man said the same exactly the thing to that same son-bitch he would act like God whispered it in his ear. I don't know what it is with the nigger and the white man. Maybe we hear the white man in 3D. He could lie to a brother and be believed. So, when I say I trusted this black man, it was real.

I used that office as a learning center, (which was my paramount objective) not to produce music, but as my own private school. I couldn't get enough of learning. The office was nice, but my goal was to learn. Don and Billy stayed in the music room from the time we opened until we closed, and honestly, I can't say what they did or wrote. I paid no attention to what they were doing. From time to time they'd ask me to come and listen, but there was nothing about them that made me think one day they would be stars. I was so backward at the time they could have had a number one song and I wouldn't have known. My only real interest was to read, and count. Higher education. I was obsessed!

Because my career started my first year in high school, what kids were going to school for I was already getting (money). But, I knew I needed help with my learning. There was no educational background in my family, but whoever would've thought a country boy like me could ever do anything; let alone need an education to learn the music business. That had never happened in my family before.

What happened to me hadn't happened yet to anyone else in black music. It was like a lost gold mine, and if I knew anything, I knew I needed help. People were running around, each one trying to get in on the ride. Every white boy who picked a guitar thought he could play and sing his way to black gold, and all of a sudden there was a swell in race music.

It was unbelievable. All the haters were now loving our music and trying to beat us to the gold mine. They heard that ting-a-ling at the cash register and that color thing didn't matter. It was business. Record studios got so blackness became invisible, and the doors to our culture and the heritage of our race music no longer mattered. The door was open and there was money in them there blues. There it was again. Let's take it from the niggers. You would've thought every white boy who sounded like somebody and had a black attitude could do it better than the coloreds.

Before "Lawdy Miss Clawdy" there was only one radio station in America that played black music with any kind of regularity and that was WLAC in Nashville, Tennessee. It seemed like after that song white boys from everywhere were trying to sound black. Even on the radio. Can you imagine? They even gave themselves black show names: Moon Man, Hound Dog, Poppa Stoppa, Dr. Daddyo, and even a dog food name, The Gravy Train Show with the Wolf Man. It worked so well that getting my education became even more important.

With the onslaught of white boys entering the blues business, I began to notice that our black humility and conditioning to serve the master was setting in once again. We were tricked by our need to feel included, and we taught them how to play our music, you could say, for free. We actually gave it away for scale.

For those of you who don't know what scale is, scale is what a musician gets for his or her service to play their instrument at a recording session. The session lasts say, two and a half hours, and the pay at the time, let's say, was one hundred dollars. What happened when the white entrepreneur came into the business and tried to duplicate the black sound with white musicians who couldn't play it, the fastest way to get to the head of the line was to mix the artist and white band into the rhythm section with some black musicians.

For instance, a black drummer and bass player might be paired with a white singer like Bobby Darin. To keep them happy, the white producer paid the black musicians double scale, and it worked. Now, the two blacks who played on the record got in demand. In the business it's called hot. That combination worked so well for them with white singers, that single scale was no longer sufficient for black musicians to play on black records. It was now double to triple scale, plus cab fare.

I begged the black musicians not to do it. Don't turn your backs on the black artists. They can't afford to pay double scale. Their companies won't allow it for the black artist. But, these black musicians were the best at what they did. The black record company couldn't pay, and that's when the cat was let out of the bag. The black musicians gave the secret of making hit records away for scale, and there weren't a whole lot of "them." But the few there were, lived in the studio with the white boys. It was the record session musicians that caused the crash of black music.

My plea to these musicians in New Orleans, and New York, was to keep the artist for yourselves. I didn't have to be a genius to see what was going on. It wasn't that complicated. Let us just keep the music for ourselves. I had a record label. Let's use it. But instead, they gave it away for peanuts. A whole industry gave music away for scale.

Why is it that black men don't hear each other? Most of them were not paying attention to what was going on. More recently, Ray Charles or Stevie Wonder could've seen that shit coming. It was the end of the rainbow, the end of the black gold, and for them it was over. There were no more good players for a single scale session for blacks, so there were no more black stars. That made it even more important that I learned how to do this business.

My generation of Negro musicians who were in show business had to be the dumbest group of niggers ever lived. The whole new music industry was ours for the taking, and we sold it for bullshit, for triple scale to the highest white bidder. Those of us who tried to save it for ourselves nearly got blackballed out of the business by the white labels, and all kinds of crap attached to our names. We were called gangsters, but in the real sense, whatever in the world would make a white man call a nigger a gangster?

Later, I learned that it was all done by design. That really got my attention and that's the one place where I absolutely give the white man an "A" for genius. He really knew how to fool a nigger. What did he have to tell that black guy to have him believe that we musicians and artists were gangsters, and that he was a gangster, too? You have to give the white man credit. He saw he was winning, as he had the niggers plotting against each other when they should have been working together. The hired nigger knew the white man, his boss, was lying when he talked about another nigger. But, he took it as the truth and went out to play gangster, beating up on singers and musicians who were his boss's competition.

I saw two hundred and fifty pounds of a black goon who worked for Morris Levy's Roulette Records beat the shit out of Tommy Hunt of the Flamingos in a phone booth at the Apollo Theater in New York. You might remember Tommy's voice on The Flamingo's hit "Human." Not only did the goon run Tommy away from the group, he ran him out of the country. The last time I saw Tommy was a few years back in an airport in Nairobi, Kenya in Africa.

That should tell you how much a black knew about being a gangster. Gangsterism was more than going around beating up singers. Gangsterism shut down black music and put it to sleep. It was no longer fun going to radio stations with these goons sitting at the door. When a white executive couldn't get a record played on a radio station that had black

DJs, they'd send these goons disguised as promotion men with instruction to get the records played, no matter what. The black program director was scared shitless and often hired his own protection. The goons, however, had their own play book, and used cocaine, cash money, or an ass whipping, whatever it took to get the job done.

Can you imagine the power that nigger felt? And, just think how smooth that white man was to pull that off with that dumb, fake, gangster nigger. The white man was very shrewd and got his record heard. It blows my mind, just the thought of it, and not one of those niggers knew how he screwed up black music. Every law authority in the country was looking for the suckers who were playing gangster, yet they had no idea what they were doing. Being sent to beat up DJs in the black radio stations was only the beginning. Yep, the white man won and the result was our end.

Didn't the nigger know the real gangsters? The Irishman who ran the police department and the hospital? The Jews who ran the courts and the education systems? The Italian who ran the waterfronts, unions, and sanitation departments? The Chinaman who ran the gangs, Chinatown, and the drugs? And the white man, of course, who sat in congress with a bought ticket for the seat he held, and in the courthouses the guy in his black robe that ran them all? Did he not know that? Money was the poisonous fruit. So what made the nigger who went around beating up entertainers and disc jockeys think he was a gangster when his boss had to give him bus fare?

As far as I know the only two blacks who stood up to try to keep black music and didn't need to was Harold Logan (my partner), and me. Harold was a West Virginia numbers man who had been my promoter since my first record. He also was a dance promoter and we got to be friends. I thought he was smart, so I asked him be a partner with me. To my surprise, he gave up his own business to help me when I opened my office in New York.

It was during my second wave of hits that I closed the office in DC and set up in the music building at 1650 Broadway, right in the heart of New York City. In 1959 I was the number one recording artist in America, so the move was to satisfy my status. You can't be big and small at the same time, and to me being big meant New York. Logan agreed and came with me.

Because Logan was a loyal friend and helped me get started again, I changed the name of my publishing company to Lloyd and Logan Music, and when blacks were selling out we stood up and tried to help some of them. Some were artists whose names I won't mention here. It certainly doesn't matter now; all the damage was done. But, we reached out to help them help themselves. It didn't matter though. The black music craze was over.

By 1963, my contract was ending with ABC-Paramount Records, which was the last time I gave them a record to release. I had a three-year deal and was the lone black rock/blues artist there. The relationship started when AMPAR (same company as ABC-Paramount, just a different name) distributed my KRC label. Before that, they had just one other record of mine "Just Because." I made that company millions and a name. So much so that no other black face came to ABC, other than Johnny Nash ("I Can See Clearly Now" 1972), without me getting a call from Sam Clark, the president, to okay them.

This was true even when they signed or hired music producer Clarence Avant (the godfather of black music), blues legend B.B. King, or soul/funk/ R&B artist and producer Curtis Mayfield with his group, the Impressions. All later became super stars for the label.

"Among Lloyd's accomplishments is the significant role he played in integrating African American musical artists into the mainstream."
eurweb.com

Then it happened, almost like Art Rupe at Specialty. One day Sam Clark called me to his office and offered me five hundred thousand dollars to leave my foolish ideas of owning my own music business alone and get rid of that "gangster bastard" Harold Logan before he ruined my career. Sam's words shocked me. Harold, according to Sam, was a thug and didn't know shit about the music business. If I wanted to get renewed by ABC, that was the deal.

Sam was Jewish and I really liked him, but at that moment I wanted to kick his ass. How dare he talk to me like that when I helped make his company successful?

Let me tell you this. Harold Logan was no gangster. He was my best friend and to call my partner a gangster was to call me one, too. It was all because we believed they cheated, fudged on the number of records I actually sold, and we called them on it. I was not having it. If looking out for my interest made Harold Logan a gangster, then so be it. All he did was make sure I got paid fairly.

Nowhere in our relationship had Sam ever called me a friend. Not once did he offer me one thing, and now he wanted to protect me from Harold Logan? Where did that come from? All I had ever been to him was a money machine. He never invited me to his house for dinner and I'd been to Logan's house too many times to remember. I'd even cooked there. What Sam wanted was to control my music, being that I was the "last of the Mohicans."

"Sam," I said, "don't ever again make the mistake of telling me who my friends should be. If getting rid of Logan is the only way you can renew my contract, then you can take that five hundred thousand and stuff it. My loyalty and integrity are worth a lot more than money. You can't buy me like that, and the only reason you're calling Logan a gangster is because he wants you to be fair with me, like you are with the other big record stars. Why aren't you calling Alan Freed, Murray the K (Murray Kaufman), Dick Clark, and all the rest of them money-grubbing gangsters, too? Not a single white name has been mentioned by any of you, and you know that's where the problems are, the real payola crew. It certainly isn't Logan who is the gangster. One way or the other those guys got the money, their artist money, but if it makes you feel good to call Logan a gangster then go ahead, but I'm outta here."

Here's a honky I made rich. I'd single handedly made him millions, yet he didn't think I had enough sense to pick or know my friends.

15
My First Hope

In the midst of all the music industry crap, I found I needed some clarity. The way I eventually discovered myself was through the words of the Honorable Elijah Muhammad. By the 1960s he was on the scene and delivering a message that was different from anything I had ever heard. I had never heard anything positive about being black. I didn't know what he was: a preacher, a prophet, or a poet, but what was clear to me was that he was delivering a different message. I would later learn he was the US leader of the Religious Nation of Islam, but I never learned why it was called a nation.

The Honorable Elijah Muhammad's message was different from that of the Baptist or other protestant religions. The white man may not have been listening when Muhammad spoke, but we blacks were, and because of him we were singing a different tune. He told us that blacks were the "original" man, and that the "evil" whites were an offshoot race. He embedded thoughts like that in us, and all the while it was getting harder for us as a people to trust anything the white man said. It had been nearly two hundred years since the white man promised us forty acres and a mule. Trust is important, and we knew by now that the white man couldn't be trusted.

I guess I was the ringleader in my group of worshipers who celebrated Elijah and his prophets of Islam. I saw him as the last coming for the black man in America. There was always something to take away in his speeches, something as a black man in America that I didn't think about before I began to follow him. Although most of us were too afraid to say it (and I'm guilty of that as well) but we all felt in our hearts that Muhammad was the truth and the *man*!

With the bad experiences I had as a black man traveling on the road in this country, with any white face who'd talk to me like I was nothing, I couldn't say anything back for fear of losing my life. A lifetime of choking on fear, I was now front and center, drinking in every word Muhammad spoke. For the first time in my life here was a little black man who spoke like a giant, and without any fear of the earth god. He said things I had held in my heart for so many years about the white man, words I had damn near choked on.

For the first time in my life a man was saying that we were somebody, regardless of what the white man said. "But *you* first have to believe that you are somebody," he said. "Believe that above all else. When you respect yourself everyone will respect you."

He told us to dress not to kill, but to be seen, and stressed wearing a suit and tie everyday to show the world that we, too, have dignity and pride. "Put a turban on your head so you can stand out and be recognized. Don't be afraid to be who you are. Let them see you."

I ate those words like they were honey and flapjacks. And it wasn't just me. Many artists who had experienced road torture from redneck state troopers on the highway felt the same pain as I did. It was such a relief to hear someone talk about it; it was like recovering from a heart attack. Joe Tex, Jackie Wilson, Sam Cooke, Lynn Hope, Miles Davis, and Dakota Stanton, I think we all were listening. Not a single one of us had missed a bad experience from that white earth god on the road, and listening to Elijah Muhammad was a real awakening.

Muhammad not only did it for me and the other artists, but also for the thousands of pimps, junkies, and whores. Even the so-called black Baptist preachers and black community leaders were listening. Yes, everybody was listening. Muhammad made us realize that we were somebody and that we were free. Maybe not by the white man's standards, but regardless of what the white man said, we were free. Muhammad said not to let him cage our spirit because our life had just as much meaning and worth as any of God's creatures. Living was worth fighting for and you can't live in a cage and be free.

How those words helped me, even though I had never believed or understood anything less. From the time I was a small boy, I had tried to figure out why so many of us didn't think something different, other than what we were taught by the white man.

Muhammad taught us to do whatever it took to be what we thought we were. But, I had never allowed myself that luxury. My parents were always afraid that I would be the one the gowned men would catch. I was too sassy and too smart.

"Never talk back to white people, boy; they'll kill you," was something I heard over and over in my youth. I just never understood trying to be less than what I thought I was. Listening to The Honorable Messenger's tape in my car religiously gave me the strength and confidence to believe in myself. It also made me realize there was nothing to fear, because if you live in fear you're already living dead, just in an unsealed grave.

The Honorable Elijah Muhammad was like a breath of fresh spring air when he spoke. Here was a man who I didn't even know saying things I wish my father had said.

These were things I was feeling inside, but too afraid to say, and I know I wasn't alone. In fact, I'm sure there was hardly a black man in America who didn't feel like I felt, but to say it could have meant your life was over. The sad part about it was you would have given it all for the ones who loved you the most, just for trying to make a stand as a man. They would have suffered, but Elijah said, "If you don't stand for something you'll fall for anything." I'm sure he was not the first to say that, but coming out of his mouth it had a real meaning for me. And he was right. You're only allowed to die once, so be sure you stand for something.

There was nothing more certain to me than his words after I left Georgia with my new car. Things I'd always felt and believed in my heart, finally there was another voice where I might've had doubts. Back then we blacks weren't even called Americans. We were of no consequence, of zero value to the white man, the son-bitch we gave our life to as his personal slave.

During my first trip to Texas in my new car I had Muhammad's tape playing. I was just south of Killeen, Texas and knew when I passed a police car parked with its lights out on the side of the road that it wouldn't be long before he was in my rearview mirror. That time of morning I always thought they were only looking for one thing, niggers in cars. They'd park in such a way that their car headlights shone through the window and picked out who was in the car. When a car passed them in a speed zone of twenty-five miles an hour, they'd flip their lights on. It was the easiest way they could grab you, under the blanket of darkness.

There were several speeding cars ahead of me, but as soon as we went by this car pulled out and followed me and my band. It wasn't just the southern state police who did that. Pick a state anywhere in America. If you were black, it was a death trap. North, south, east, or west, they all did it for no reason at all. And, what made it worse, here you were a full-grown man and you couldn't talk back, not even to answer the question, not until he said so.

Now I was once again being confronted. I was helpless in front of a white man with a gun. The only thing that could help me or kill me would be my courage to make a stand.

"Oh, shit," one of my band members said. "If they stop us, they gonna put our asses in jail. That man in Savannah was right. We're riding with dead tags. Oh, man, they turned on their damn lights!"

In panic I said, "Everybody, put your turbans on. I'll do all the talking. Nobody else say shit!" I slowly pulled over and stopped, and this big Texas state trooper rolled out of his car. Funny, cops all seemed bigger at night. He came up to the window.

"Boy, did you see the speed limit?"

"Yes, sir."

"Give me your license and the papers to this car," he demanded with a big Texas drawl.

I just stared at him, figuring the only way out of this was to play stupid and say nothing. That was one advantage we had over them. They all thought we were stupid. So, I pretended not to understand. Instead, I said a few words in Japanese and he looked at me like I was crazy. I didn't know what else to do to protect myself, other than put my turban on so he'd think I was something other than American. I had learned to speak some Japanese when in Japan during the war, and felt I needed to say anything other than "yassuh, boss." I knew I had a chance right away when I saw he was puzzled by what I said. I was so scared I could hear my own heart beat.

Finally he said, "Boy, did you understand what I said?"

I looked at him and decided to speak a little more Japanese, only this time with a big, broad smile. As soon as I finished, his partner in the car asked, "What's going on over there John? What'd he say, and what's that on their heads? Turbans? Is it some kind of religion? You keep asking questions. They don't speak English?"

"I don't think so."

"No shit! They ain't no real niggers?"

"I don't think so. I can't get a word outta this one."

"Go take a look at the tag, John, and see what it say. What's the year on it?"

The trooper looked down at the tag. "Nineteen fifty six-seven. Hell, it could be expired."

"Where they from?"

"Uh . . . looks like the District of Columbia."

"Where's that? South America?"

At that point I knew I had them, so I smiled and made a sign like being hungry. Chop, chop.

John said to his partner, "Bill, it looks like they wanna eat. What'll we do 'bout that? Everything's closed in Nigger Town."

"Well, they ain't no niggers. If they were they'd understand us. Hell, it's late. Let's take 'em to the café in the bus station and let 'em eat shit. I'm tired anyway. Ain't nobody gonna bother 'em as long as we're there, and besides, they ain't from round here so nobody's gonna see 'em again anyway."

"Yeah, I guess we can do that. Just have them keep them turbans on."

I knew then that you can learn a lot if you pay attention.

Elijah Muhammad's words were the first truth I'd ever heard about the white man. Just the way you look makes a difference. He said something to the effect of, "Nothing white is going to fly through the sky and save you, so get up off your knees and look behind your back, because all you'll get with your head down is a cracked skull." How many of us are guilty of believing the man that enslaved us is going to send his god to save us?

Elijah had no wings and he didn't wear white, he just told us to get up. Hearing his words was like the key that let my brain out of prison. What a relief that was. I had believed, as my mother and father believed, that one day the spirit of the angels would come and let my soul out to be free. That, I now knew, was a myth. I was already free. I just hadn't believed it. To me the words of Elijah were like a miracle. This was especially true when he said in order to be somebody you have to act like somebody.

In this case the turbans on our heads made us "somebody" in that white cop's eyes. He didn't know that his whole life he'd harbored an attitude about us as black people. Now that attitude had him stumped. What should he do with a car full of niggers?

At the bus station we were treated like we belonged, even if we did sit in the back of the room. It was around three or four in the morning. In some states back then blacks were allowed to go to the counter to order. You placed your order and stepped away until you were called to pick it up.

I'd had no experience such as that in Texas, and what surprised me more than anything was how easy it was to make them believe I was something other than what I was. That proved a thing or two to me. It was all about perception, his perception. The turban gave me another look and even though my face was black he didn't hear the normal voice of a colored man that went with the face. They didn't care what I was, as long as I wasn't a traditional Negro.

This happened around the time the world was starting to change, when the British stepped down to give Ghana back to the Ghanaian people. Kwame Nkrumah, a black man, was the first president of the country and that news was not a secret. For the first time, we too, were quietly celebrating Africa. Our time was coming! The Honorable Elijah Muhammad was asking that North Carolina be dedicated as land for a black state, and here two Texas gun-toting cowboys took us conked-headed niggers with turbans for some food in a white establishment because I spoke broken Japanese. Yes, things were changing.

In addition to problems with the police, during that period in America, in the fifties and sixties, the Ku Klux Klan operated with anonymity in most towns and communities throughout the south—and in some places farther north. In many cities, as you entered, signs read THE KU KLUX KLAN WELCOMES YOU. It varied from city to city, but none read, ALL ARE WELCOMED. All would know what that meant if you were a person of color.

We knew exactly what the Klan "welcome" meant. It meant the head of the Klan might be the head of the church, the mayor, the doctor, the fire chief, or the chief of police. In towns headed by the Klan, where would a black man go for help? Nowhere. The earth god had all that covered. We had nowhere to run and nowhere to hide. Our church was our only shelter. With all that fear and nowhere to go, was our goose cooked?

There did come a time when all the elders in the black church in my town thought we might be making progress when a black man was selected for the police force, but his authority was limited. If he did anything other than clean the station it was the best-kept secret in the town.

I'm talking of times when a black policeman saw a white man robbing a bank he had no power to stop or arrest him. If he touched that man, in all probability his ass would have been arrested for acting like he was a policeman—or he may even have been shot or lynched. So who was he protecting? Certainly not us. We called him the spy. He was a "Tom" for the master.

Elijah made me think about the white man like I never had before. The man is a coward, he'd say. But wait. Think about that. Elijah Mohammad said the earth god was a *coward*! Back then do you know what would have happened if a black man called a white man a coward? Who had such nerve? Elijah did. The white man had done so much to us that he'd never let himself be caught alone with a group of niggers. He had so much fear that he wouldn't let a black officer carry a gun or ride in the same car with him.

I still believe today that if a white officer has to go to a black man's house, he'll take more officers with him. He won't go alone, and if there's the least resistance, he may handcuff him or shoot him for no reason. Could that behavior be left over from the Ol' Jakes of my past?

What always amazed me when it came to blacks and their rights, no matter what happened to the black man in the courts, he didn't win there either. With an army of whites whipping his ass they'd put their hands on a bible and swear he started the fight with handcuffs on. Courts in many cases will find a black man guilty because they assume he is lying. What kind of guts does it take to beat a man with cuffs on, and then lie about it.

There have been many times since my boyhood that I have wondered what is it that gives the white man that false sense of power? Is it that dark skin brings out a rage in him to kill the nigger? Or could it be like Ol' Jake said, that we're only half human and should be treed? Is that it?

Over the years there's been talk among white people that we should go back to Africa. Is it because we breed like wildflowers and with all he does he hasn't managed to kill us off? Does he fear we'll out breed him and someday overtake him? What comfort would he have being a minority? And, what comfort must he feel now, knowing this is coming and going to happen. Suppose he gave us free labor for hundreds of years like we gave him, with not one inkling of appreciation for his contributions?

I'm not saying this ought to happen. I'm just saying suppose. Do you think the white man will learn like we did that those who expect nothing are never disappointed? We expected nothing for our labor and nothing is what we got. And you, white man, you didn't disappoint us.

16
You Taught Me

For a while I must admit that things did start getting a little foggy. It felt like something was wrong, something was missing in my life. I was acting white, getting my nappy hair processed, and dating white women. All that white stuff became like snow and all those blond, blue-eyed women started to melt together in my mind. The wine even began to taste bad and I couldn't hear the songs anymore.

I realized I wanted to go back across the tracks. Even though I didn't want to leave my life of luxury, I thought a visit might be a good idea. I'd go to the barbershop to hear the latest, to feel something like home, but then my white girlfriend and her jealous heart wanted to go with me. That was a drag because the word was already out that I was a honky lover. No matter what street I walked down with my white woman, I saw and felt the look of resentment on the faces of both black women and white men. It was a look of wanting to cut my throat. Why? Because I was living a dream. Then it hit me. Good dreams often have bad endings.

When I tried to bend the rules by being with the opposite color partner, the natural feeling outside the bedroom was not so great for me. Many times I asked myself the question *what am I doing here*? Everything in me told me I was in the wrong place because I couldn't neutralize feelings and make something out of what it wasn't.

It's much better to try and be an American, than trying to be white. I tried it, and it didn't work. It didn't work for me on the black side nor did it work on the white, so it shouldn't be something you go around acting like and faking. It's a bold step, and for me, being around white women and acting like I felt great about that, was uncomfortable.

If you are honest with yourself, you must see this picture. At your white wife or white girlfriend's house on a holiday (if she's allowed to bring you) you have to know that somebody in that household did not agree to have you there. Her friends probably don't know she is with a black man. If they do, I bet they're wondering what is she thinking. There's a good chance the people there never met you, and there're going to be totally surprised to see you there. Forget all the fake smiles and handshakes. Whatever the affair might be, you must know you're going to be the spoiler for everybody.

Some clichés are true. That fly in the bowl of milk ruins the whole bowl. So don't be white if you're not. You'll never be accepted as one of them. You're still black and that is best for you. Don't pretend to be what you're not; then you can go back across the tracks without the embarrassment of your color.

I wonder if white people feel that way when they're with their black lovers? I felt on the edge of being embarrassed all the time. But just suppose I didn't have those feelings of color, and they didn't either, and we were all just plain American?

Women aside, the only way I can describe my success during the time I had all those hit records, was that in my mind I was big, right up there with the likes of people such as the famed banker and financier J.P. Morgan. I almost felt like smoking cigars. The money was coming so fast I thought birds were flying it in through the windows. It did make me feel like something I wasn't.

Really, it was sickening. It seemed every time the phone rang somebody wanted to give me money, and that was a problem. The only reason I got love and invites was because of my fame and success. I knew it was never about me the person. There's nothing new when you're riding high, except that everybody wants a seat on the bus. But what was more sickening than all of that was I didn't know what to do with it, or who to be. I didn't have the first idea. I knew more about faking being a white man than I knew about money. That was an area where the need to teach us finance was never felt to be necessary where we lived in southern Louisiana. And you know what? None of our families had money problems, because they didn't have any money.

Whoever thought a little black boy from Kenner, Louisiana would one day be rich? I didn't know how to play the rich kid with any measurable amount of believability, even though I was told by my "boys" I was. Never did I have dreams about having money. How could I know anything about it? My advisors told me to buy bonds, it was the safest investment, and that investing in bonds would make me a credible person at the bank, whatever that meant. They could've said anything and it would've sounded good to me. It's a bitch when you don't know. But, I was *big* and the money I was making at that time was very big. You could say I was "poor man's rich."

The advice about money had come from my white lawyers in New York. They also said I should do something with the money, as the amount we were talking about was a little over a half million dollars. That was a huge amount of money in the 1950s. I was doing a lot of one-night stands and was paid in cash, and I kept a lot of the money in five hundred and thousand dollar bills in my car. I don't have to tell you how surprised they were that no one had taken it. Anyway, they convinced me to put some of the money in bonds, and to let my attorney, Andy Feinman, open an escrow account at the bank for me with the rest. That sounded good to me.

Now, bear in mind that I'm *big*. You can't be big and small at the same time, but I was living a black man's dream in a white man's world in New York. In no way did I want them to know I was really stupid. I left that meeting and my money with Andy, and I felt comfortable doing it. He had been my attorney all of six months, but that never phased me because I was too busy being one of *them*. Big. I'd let my attorney invest my money.

Here's the hook. I didn't even know which bank he was using to put my money in. Can you imagine? If the day hadn't come when I needed some money I probably still wouldn't know the name of the bank. And, if he was dead and gone that might have been when I realized how stupid it was to trust a son-bitch I did not even know. Lawyer or not, I got upset when it hit me that I didn't know this man.

Slick shit slips up on you when people sense you're listening to stuff you know nothing about and are trying to be something that you're not.

Before I knew it, my shit was down the tubes. I had never gotten a checkbook and I knew that was wrong. It was my money. I got on the phone, and boy was I mad!

"Where's my checkbook, Andy? Where's my money?"

"Lloyd, my man," he said. "How're you're doing? What can I help you with?"

"You never sent me a checkbook for the money."

"Oh, the money," he said. "That money."

"Yeah, my money," I said. "The money I left with you."

"Lloyd my man, for a minute you had me thinking something was wrong. Don't you remember what we discussed? I bought a couple hundred thousand in bonds and the rest I put in the bank."

"What bank?" I asked. "That's why I'm calling. I don't know anything about the whereabouts of the bread, and I gotta have some."

"Well, Lloyd, you know all you have to do is ask. Have I ever let you down?"

"Just a moment!" I said. "What do you mean, ask? I want the checkbook and the certificate for the bonds."

"Well Lloyd, I didn't do it like that. You told me to handle it so there's no checkbook for you. The deal was for me to save your money and the best way I thought to do that was to put it in escrow, so it's in my escrow account. Didn't you look at the statement I sent you? It's all there."

"I don't wanna look at no statement, I need my money."

Then to add insult to injury, he asked how much I needed. That didn't go to my white side at all. I was feeling my black side war paint coming out in my face, but I managed to stay cool. He had my money. It took some time but I got that shit straight, otherwise you wouldn't be reading this now because I'd be somewhere in prison.

What I learned from that experience was that lawyers often put client money in escrow accounts but I did not have the business savvy to know that. I, like a lot of black people was too trusting and did not have the facts I needed. A nigger would trust a white truck driver with brain surgery before he'd let a brother put a band-aid on his finger. I know that son-bitch attorney wouldn't loan me a dime if my life depended on it, and I had trusted him with all that bread. Yes, I can see the position he took as my lawyer. He was showing me how to save my money in the bank, but in his bank account. Can you believe that?

Still green behind the ears, I had all the money put into an account with my name on it, but at the same bank. I just don't know what it is that makes us so soft that a white man can talk us into anything. Why do we think he knows everything?

At that time I had no idea how strong my money made Andy at the bank, and I couldn't get a nickel bottle of Coca-Cola. Why didn't he tell me what he had done? I'm a good listener. I heard everything else he said. He could've told me anything and it would have been all right. Just don't tell me I'm colored and my understanding is different. I must admit I was guilty of believing in white people, but on the other hand, who and what was there to compare to? There was no one. I must say, as difficult a time as that was, each one of those hard days was a part of an important learning process.

17
No Friends in the Bank for Blacks

When I finally got wise to what Andy was doing, all my juices really started to flow. My tutor, Bill Boskent, told me I should use Andy like he was trying to use me. He said I should use the influence that Andy got from my money and have him go to the bank and borrow money for me. That way I could use the bank's money and let mine sit.

After Bill explained what all that meant, I had Andy do just that. With all the money I had at that bank I shouldn't have a problem borrowing funds for my business, and I shouldn't have a problem with credit, because I never had any. The deal was to ask the bank for fifty thousand dollars and to use my bonds for collateral. Andy saw no problem with that and I saw it as a real plus, because it would establish me as a serious and reliable bank customer.

Being a bit naïve, I didn't know that I was probably the first black man in his early twenties who ever tried to borrow fifty thousand dollars from a bank in the late fifties or early sixties. My dad's house cost eight hundred dollars not long before that and I was trying to borrow fifty thousand. We went to the bank and gave all the documents to the bank manager for the loan.

Actually, Andy gave them to him. I sort of sat there and grinned while all kinds of stuff went off in my head. I was a country boy from Kenner, Louisiana asking a New York bank to loan me fifty thousand dollars. I was *big* and that was a big deal, especially since not that long ago I was working for a soda pop, a fish sandwich, and five bucks. This was sure e-nuff high cotton.

If the loan went through it would mark the first turn around I had with a white boy where he'd earned his fee. That was the other reason I didn't cut Andy loose. I needed him. There I was in New York, new in this business, and there were more white people than I had ever seen. There was a need for him, or somebody like him, so I was glad to have him.

Andy was my new agent, as well as Tim Gales's attorney. Tim Gales was the owner of the biggest black booking agency in the country. He also had a lot of success with Gales Music Publishing. With a welcome to his office, Andy gave me a new car for signing. I was his new head nigger and Tim had said Andy was all right. That was cool with me up to a point, because I was still learning, but I was willing to bend a little and give him a shot, because Tim said so.

In the month that followed I spoke to Andy several times about the loan, and he'd tell me not to worry, that these things take time. Fair enough, I could wait, but in the mean time I couldn't believe that here I was, in my twenties, with more money than my father could ever imagine. As a matter of fact, I doubted that my father had ever been in a bank. Where we're from, the first bank had just opened, built and converted from an old used car garage. Black people had no reason to go there. I know my father didn't. We called it that "white bank" on the highway.

After a month or so Andy finally called and asked me to meet him at the bank. The bank manager had some information about the loan. A cold chill ran through me at that news. I didn't realize how excited I was at the prospect of having credibility at the bank, since a bank was the gauge that says who you are. Bill Boskent said, "If you get the loan, you're going to be a real man now, Clawdy." I didn't know exactly what he meant, him being half white, but he said I had all the right qualifications so there'd be no reason to be turned down. I must admit I was hyped.

When I got to the bank the manager took us to a huge conference room and sat at a table that looked large enough to seat seventy-five people. It was like being in a courtroom, and the mere size of it was intimidating. As he sat across from us he pulled out a folder with some papers. The next words from his mouth were, "we have a problem."

I'd already figured that out just from being in that big ass room. Then he spoke directly to Andy, as if I wasn't sitting there. First he said he was surprised at the outcome. "But, you know how the banking business is," he said with a little smile on his face.

Andy knew me a hell of a lot better than the bank manager did. He knew I knew white code when someone is talking "pass the nigger." Plus, the manager never looked at me once, which was a sure give away.

"It's like this," said the manger. "We ran a check on Mr. Price and we couldn't find anything on him good or bad, and in banking that's not good. There is no way to make a judgment on his credit, so with no history we had no choice but to turn down the application."

"Ah, come on John, be honest with us," Andy said. "Was that the reason? The man's got over half a million dollars sitting in this bank, so your fifty's covered."

"No Andy, that's not altogether true. We went over that and the consensus was that indeed he has the money to cover the loan, which brought us to this point. If he has the money, why does he have to borrow? And there's another point. Although the money is here right now, he can take it whenever he wants, and this bank needs something a little more solid than that. Plus, he's an entertainer. That doesn't represent steady employment, which is another strike against him."

"Let's stop the bullshit John," Andy said. "Did color have anything to do with the board's decision? Do they know he's a black man and did they use that against him?"

"Yes," John said, "and that was the major problem. I'm sorry you asked, but that was it. There was no way I could convince the board that this was a brand new day and a man's business shouldn't have anything to do with the color of his skin."

At last he looked at me, "Mr. Price, you were well covered for the loan but it was the color of your skin they turned down, and you have to forgive me but it's a fucking shame, and that sucks."

Andy and I just looked at each other. Neither one of us said a word because we both knew if I was a white boy with that kind of money in the bank the whole board would be out here kissing my ass to get my business. It was clear to me, though. If I made all the money in the world it would've been the same no matter what. The smallest thing a white man ever saw was a big nigger, and I was big.

When the bank manager said he didn't understand why the bank board was so prejudiced the first thing that came to my mind was to get him some glasses and send the board a mirror. But as sure as shooting, the next month I got Andy's bill for the meeting at the bank. The beat goes on!

One day just thinking about it I got so pissed that I went to the bank to get all my money out. I didn't want anything to do with that bank and I said to the bank manager, "Give me all my money right now!"

"Mr. Price, we don't keep that kind of cash on hand. I'll have to order it for you."

Well that really fired me up. "What the hell? You mean you don't have my money?"

"Please, if you just be patient, I'll get your money. Why are you so emotional?"

That is what that man said to me. Why was I so emotional? That question almost put me in shock. I don't recall how he did it, but I felt stupid. I was like that fly in the bowl of milk in that big white bank. I couldn't get my money and was told to calm down. I guess that was called "putting the nigger in his place."

I did calm down and waited for my money. When it finally came I bought a safe and kept it in my house. I learned a lot from that experience. Not only was there no accepting of the black man's business, but there also (and again) was no justice for people of color in public banking. Sadly, at that point in time, there was no law that said there had to be.

18
I'm a Nigger (I Thought)

For as long as I could remember, I image it was in my DNA, I had a dream to go to Africa. All I ever heard when I was young was that niggers were from Africa. But until I went to Africa, I had all this black and white crap screwed up.

At some point I realized there was no way I could accept or enjoy the conditions that were handed down to me here in America in the forties, fifties, and sixties. I can't tell you what it felt like not feeling welcome in my place of birth, especially when I knew no other place, spoke no other language, and knew no other culture. I'd made some money, so after thinking about it for a while I decided I would go home to Africa. This was in the 1970s.

I don't know why I expected to be greeted with open arms, like any homeboy or cousin. Maybe it was because I was told so often that Africa was my home. My excitement when I finally got to Africa, when I finally came home, was overwhelming. I couldn't wait to get off the plane in Nigeria to get the real story, the low down, of how my people were kidnapped in the middle of the night, hog tied, and brought to America against their will. I picked Nigeria because they spoke English, and I wanted to know what happened to my people in words I understood. Consequently, I got off that plane madder than a bitch, ready to hear the real story on the white man. I was fired up!

You can't imagine what it felt like to put my foot on African soil for the first time. I was home. I was finally in a place that every other race of people on earth had known forever, a place they called home, the Motherland. Pick any culture—French, German, Irish, Italian, English, Chinese, Japanese, Arabic, or Jewish—all had somewhere to land on Mother Earth and be sons and daughters of the soil.

I knew I wasn't going to be satisfied until I got there too, to my homeland, to Africa. This was no "pie in the sky or get your ribbon when you die" crap, this was the real deal. Home. I wanted "the cookie on the ground while I was around" and I was so happy. I had dreamed of Africa for a long, long time and the amazing thing was, when I got there all I saw was black people. I had never been anyplace where black was all I saw. Along with my righteous anger I was so happy when I got off the plane I kissed the ground and tears welled in my eyes. Finally, I was with my people. True freedom at last!

Long before I ever thought of going to Africa, I told my friends I'd rather live in a shithouse in Africa than in a mansion in Mississippi. It would be impossible for me to tell you how much joy I felt in my heart being there, it was like when my wife gave birth to my first child. I was a happy son-bitch.

But, before I could ask the first question about my bloodline and my family village, all the joy left me, instantly, like a rocket taking off for the moon. Talk about niggers with attitudes! If I tell you I was welcomed and they were happy to see me, that would be a lie. In Lagos, the largest city in Nigeria, before I could get to the gate it was robbery in a uniform. It was such a shock to me that I was speechless. These were some mean niggers with attitudes, and the only English they spoke was, "dash," "quarantine," "give me some money," or "you can't come in." What was this, a stick up?

At first I didn't get what they meant by dash. I finally learned that dash meant if you didn't give them, say, five hundred dollars, you'd be threatened with quarantine, meaning you couldn't get in the country. Instead, you'd be locked up at the gate. How was that for a welcome after flying for a full day and half the night?

I've never been nobody's ass kisser but once I saw what Africa was about, right there at the gate, I wanted to find that white man or whoever started slavery and thank him for getting my family out of there. After I saw that crap I wanted to kiss the slave masters, just to show my appreciation. This was some dumb shit and if there had been a boat leaving right then, I knew I'd be the first one on the boat, rather than continue through immigration, because this was beginning to look like the lost wild world. I already knew the drill on the slave ship from the history of the slaves. I'd have put the chain around my own neck and the nail in my own lips just to get out of there.

But, I did want to keep my airline return ticket as a reminder not to ever have that dream again. I had never seen anything like it, the way those son-bitches talked and looked at me. I thought the white man was frightening. But these niggers made Ol' Jake look like an angel.

A big, blue-black lipped nigger took my passport, and with the hiss of a rattlesnake ordered me to go with him to the back. In broken English he sounded worse than a Texas redneck and treated me just as bad. In real broken speech he told me I didn't clear immigration properly.

"Let's go to the back," he said.

"To the back, where?" I asked.

"To the back," he ordered. This was one angry dude.

I followed him around a junk pile that seemed a mile high. It looked and smelled like the city dump.

"Come, come," he demanded sharply. "Now!"

I wondered why he had such a bad attitude.

In a little room in the back, he sat before me, just like that white judge in Mississippi had. It was the same kind of intimidation, only this time it came from a black man, and that felt stranger than you could imagine.

"Your passport is not stamped correctly."

"What's wrong with the stamp?" I asked.

"Oh, brotha, nuthin' much," he said with a smile on his face. "We can work this out. You dash me money; I will let you go. No problem, okay? Otherwise I will have to hold you right here, in quarantine, and then send you back to the states."

"Ain't shit wrong with that stamp," I snapped. "It was stamped and approved at your embassy."

"No, no," he said. "It is not stamped properly. You must pay entrance fee in Nigeria."

I could see I was being had and that there was no way out. "So, how much, you three-lip fucker?"

"Oh, five hundred US, okay?" Then he looked at me curiously. "What's a three-lip fucker?" he asked.

"You don't want to know," I replied, trying to restrain my anger.

At that moment I finally realized where the terms slick nigger and bullshit came from. My ancestral cousin, the originator of bullshit, had to be African. He'd also be the biggest shit stirrer-upper ever. Everyone would know him, but he kept his thing going because he always had a few dollars. If you needed it, he'd be the one to tell a story a mile long and none of it be true. I thought that hearing this shit from three lips here in Africa, the old slick-o at home was gonna need more practice.

It took about two hours before I was able to claim my luggage. When I got to the baggage room, which was the size of a basketball court, there must have been three or four hundred people looking for their luggage, too. It all was in one big pile. Even though I couldn't understand any of the languages I was hearing, the facial expressions of my fellow travelers told the story. There was no defined area for any of the flights, no matter where they came from. All baggage, from all flights, was thrown on the floor in a massive pile.

I went through hundreds of pieces of luggage trying to find mine, and when I finally found them they had been opened and gone through. All except a few pieces of clothing were gone. Someone had taken all my stuff and I'm still puzzled why they left what they did. What kind of homecoming was this? On top of being robbed twice before leaving the airport, no one spoke English and it was so hot in there you could almost smell yourself cooking. No country shithouse in America ever smelled that funky.

If you run into a son-bitch in America with bad breath, take it as a breath of fresh air compared to those niggers around that airport. Their breath was so bad, from a nut called cola and brushing their teeth with sticks, that their teeth had turned green. If there was a way to can that smell it could have been used to make gun power. I started asking myself what was fastest way out of this hell hole.

Thinking I had gone through the worst part of this escapade, I found out that none of these people spoke "Niggdom" either, you know, like we black folks do back home. I even tried a little pig Latin, but that didn't work either. What really messed me up, though, was that when I used the word motherfucker it seemed to have no effect. I was a lost soul. How can you call a black man a motherfucker and get no response?

In America that word is a great part of our black culture, and is very important in the language. If you call someone a word like that and he doesn't know you, you might have a fight on your hands. I was beginning to think I had lost my voice, or maybe they just couldn't hear me. I said, "You motherfuckers," as loudly as I could and those sonbitches just stood there and laughed at me in the main terminal baggage room. Then it came to me. They didn't understand me because they weren't niggers or coloreds. How could I communicate with another nigger if he didn't understand motherfucker? That was our secret code!

As if that wasn't bad enough, when I got to the outside of the terminal, dozens of those little green-teethed people surrounded me, reaching for my empty bags. They were actually taking them out of my hands. I didn't understand them and they didn't understand me. We were all fucked up. Then I thought about something I'd seen in a Hollywood movie, that half man, half animal shit, and I remembered what I had heard as a child, that the real African will eat you up. That got to me. Maybe this little army of Ubangies surrounding me was talking about dinner!! When I needed him, where was Ol' Jake with that gun?

19
Bola

Just when I thought I was doomed, the white man's god heard my prayer. It had to be his god because the black man's god must be an answering machine, as he has never answered anybody's prayer, as much as we believe such a god exists.

"Brother, let me help you," a voice behind me said.

I turned and looked into a face so black that the first thing I could think to call him was Smokey. That name was quickly followed by Smokey Red Eyes. There were no other names to fit that face—except maybe Dark, Darker, or Midnight. He spoke to the little green-teethed people in Ubangie, or some other language, and they scattered like wild rabbits, as if he had a whip in his hands. I thought he must be the police. I really didn't care who he was though, because he spoke English, and as far as I was concerned he was my man.

"I'm glad you held onto your bags, sir," he said. "If one of these people got their hands on them, chances are you'd never see them again."

Smokey surprised me after what I'd just gone through, especially with that ass in immigration. It was hard to believe that here was somebody who seemed to have some integrity.

"Man, you don't know how glad I am to hear your voice," I said. "Here I am, my first time home in over four hundred years and so far it's been a total disappointment. I came here to see if I could find any traces of my family or village but so far all I want to do is turn around and go back to the States. I've never seen so many wild son-bitches in my life, and what's that stuff they're talking?"

"My friend," Smokey said, "pay no attention to these people. They are all illiterate. Don't mind them a t'all. Let me take your bags, sir."

There must have been as many little green-teethed people outside the airport as there were in the baggage room. The only difference was everybody out here had their hands out begging for money and, if I'd had weak stomach, the smell would have made me throw up. I had never seen such people or smelled an odor as strong as that, and to say they were poor would be the understatement of my life. This made living in poverty in America look like being born into the Rockefeller family. Smokey saw the expression on my face, so to ease my concern, he spoke.

"The politicians in this country are all crooks," he said. "Look at this place. Someday I hope they take some of that money out of their pockets and clean it up. It's a real health hazard, and the children eat from dumps while those money grabbers and thieves fill their pockets. Day in and day out these poor people are here begging for food and grabbing what they can. This is all they have. Nobody cares. Nobody!

So it's very hard to blame them. You can be sure of one thing, sir, the rich in Africa gets richer and the poor gets poorer."

I was touched by his words, but it was the same everywhere. The big people never gave the little people anything more than hard times, but I did not yet fully understand, as Smokey did not look like he was one of them.

"Brother," I asked, "what is your name and what part of this country are you from?"

"My name is Bola sir. Bola Omar Bello. I'm from the north and my tribe is Hausa, the largest tribe in the north of this country. Lagos is the federal capital of our republic, and most of the people in these parts are Yoruba."

Before I got into his cab I took a good look at the physical make-up of the green-teethed people, and then looked at Bola, but couldn't tell the difference. They all looked black to me, meaning they looked alike, but this group was much smaller in weight and height and spoke a different language. Bola was a little guy with a big, godly voice who was dressed nice and was polite. He seemed to be smart, but was a taxi driver.

Curious, I asked, "Is it the same in your part of the country, Bola? Do the politicians take all the money for their pockets and leave the poor people hungry?"

"Yes, sir."

"Then you, Bola, must be a rich man," I said, "You are away from home and driving this nice car as a taxi. You must have money."

"A rich man . . . oh no, sir. This car is not mine. It belongs to my boss, who is a big man. He has many cars."

"Well, it's mighty hot in here Bola," I said, as I took my handkerchief from my pocket and wiped my face. "I can feel myself frying in here. Do you know, has the big man ever heard of air conditioning?"

Bola smiled as he started the engine. "This is Africa, sir. It is always hot here, that's why we Africans grow big lips and noses so we can breathe and keep air in our lungs. Where in the states are you from sir, New York? For my whole life I have wanted to go to America and I will go someday before I die, so help me."

My mind stopped as I took a look at Bola. Then I began to wonder if he really knew what he was saying. Had he ever thought about all the people who were kidnapped from their tribes in the middle of the night right here in Africa, my people, and tucked away in the bottom of an old wooden boat for months? They never saw the light of day, slept in feces, and rolled against dead bodies rotting in the dark, some of whom I'm sure were family, my family. These people hundreds of years ago were stolen and locked in chains and brought to America against their will. That was why I was here.

I wondered if Bola knew how badly our people are treated once they get to America? Would he still want to go? I guess the grass does look greener on the other side. Honestly, I didn't think he would be comfortable in America, just as I was not comfortable being here in Africa. Our worlds were just too far apart now.

"No, I'm not from New York and I see you don't want to talk about that air conditioner either. But I go to New York from time to time, and I see some of your big men, rich politicians, acting like a white man. They hardly ever socialize in the black circles.

"Bola, I'm from the south in America, Louisiana, where the big man is a white man and the poor people there don't call him big, they call him 'mister.' But, behind his back they call him honky, cracker, redneck, and whatever else they can think of. After going through this shit here though, maybe he should be called a 'big man.' When I get back to the states, I just might try to find him. I want to kiss him personally to thank him for making a way for my family. I'm so glad I was born out of here, and I want to thank him for not sending us back. I know you don't know what I'm talking about Bola, it's a long story." Then to change the subject, I asked. "How long is the ride to my hotel?"

"Oh, sir, this time of day we're right in the middle of the 'go slow' and it could take a while. It's only about forty kilometers but everybody has the right-of-way. There are no traffic lights in the country that work and the system is crazy the way it is set up. It operates with an odd and even tag number. Even numbers get to drive on one day and odd on the next. The problem is everybody who can afford it has two cars, so the traffic never lets up. You haven't seen traffic 'til you see the road from the Port of Apapa, through Lagos, and on north to the airport. There will be many fights from accidents along the way sir, and this will hold us up so you must have patience, because there are no police. It's all settled with a fistfight and there are no winners.

I had a feeling then that this was going to be a tough visit. "So who keeps the order Bola, if there are no policeman who run the country?"

"The soldiers, sir. They run everything, and ruin everything, too. They are very mean . . . very! So be vigilant while you're here because they will rob you, then put you in jail and frame you as a troublemaker. Be very, very careful."

"How's this hotel I'm going to?" I asked.

"The best in the country, sir. It's very safe there. You must be a big man yourself, sir, to be staying there."

"Bola, cut out that sir shit, okay? I'm just a little nigger from Louisiana who got lucky and followed a dream, like the one you have about going to America. I've always wanted to come here to Africa because I've been told all my life that this was my home. The white man, or the 'big man' as you call him has been saying that niggers like me are from Africa, so before my parents leave this earth I at least wanted them to know I had been home."

Bola took his eyes off the road than looked at me strangely. "Are you a Nigger, sir?"

At first I didn't think I'd heard him right. "Ask me that question again, Bola."

"Are you a Nigger, sir?"

"Exactly what do you mean by that?" I asked.

"Well, sir, I don't see your marks. In fact, I don't see any marks on your face. I don't think you are a Nigger sir, and you certainly don't look Sambo. And Sambos and Niggers are the two most powerful tribes in Hausa and the marks on their faces are more than worthy of high praise and royal respect. If you were either of those, your marks would have been put on at your birth. That's what I meant, sir. I would know you. It would be easy for me to tell if you were a Nigger, but maybe you are an Igbo or a Tiv man, sir. Your face has that same structure with high cheekbones and they, too, are also very respectable tribes. I don't know if you are either, sir, but you are certainly not a Nigger. But you *are* somebody, for God sent you back home to see us."

Instead of our derogatory use of the words nigger and sambo, Bola was referring to respected and ancient African tribes. In fact, what Bola probably said was Naga and Sambho. That was when I began to relax and pay attention not only to what Bola was saying but also to my surroundings. There was no way I could miss the shanties and the stench on both sides of the road. Women as well as men and children were pissing and shitting right there in front of me. It was the most terrifying sight I had ever seen.

At first I was embarrassed to see a woman pull her dress up, and show her big ass pointed at the sun and take a shit. I had never seen anything like that at home and wasn't sure how to relate to it. I didn't want to look. Maybe she was crazy or something, but then I saw another, and another, do the same thing. Then I saw men whipping their joints out and pissing on the street, and none of them seemed to care or were embarrassed. Finally, I asked.

"Bola, what are these people doing shitting on the road?

He laughed. "They are just easing themselves, sir. This is Africa. That's what we do here."

"Why don't they use bathrooms?"

"What bathrooms, sir? This is not America. We don't have bathrooms. The land belongs to all of us and we use it any way we like. Don't be embarrassed by what you see, sir."

For a while I got carried away emotionally, because it really *was* kind of embarrassing. Of all the places I'd been to in the world, I'd never seen anything like this. I remembered what I'd heard about my people being only half human, and it was beginning to make me reflect back to the railroad track crossing back home in Kenner where Ol' Jake called us half monkeys.

The only other group of living things I'd ever seen shit like this on the road were animals, and now there were groups of people, black people, peeing and pooping on the road, some of whom might even have been my kinfolk. That was enough to put a lot on my mind. I thought about Korea, and how I thought it was the asshole of the world, that you couldn't get any lower than that. Where else did people use human waste in their fields to farm and grow vegetables? I thought that was disgusting. But in Africa they didn't use the shit for anything. They just left it there for the next one to step in.

Who are these people I wondered? The only thing I had not seen so far was the African pig-man I'd heard about in my youth. I also thought by coming here I might find a trace of my family's tree, but I didn't expect to find them shitting on the side of the road. Now all of us, black and white, at one time had take a pee on the side of the road in an emergency, but that doesn't make you African or half human. What I saw, though, was no emergency. These people I saw doing it, that was their way of life. According to Bola, any place you felt it coming on you just dropped it. Let me tell you, it was very strange.

In New York people complain about doggie doo-doo in the park or on the sidewalk, but I've never heard of anyone complain about people doo-doo. I'm sure if you were caught you were going to jail, so this was a bit much, but what concerned me was there was nobody coming to pick it up. They just crapped and left it. In New York that doggie doo-doo man would pick it up eventually, when the park was cleaned.

I decided that if I had come to Africa to stay awhile, Bola most definitely would be someone I'd call a friend. His English was impeccable. In fact, I thought he sounded like an English aristocrat. I wondered what other language he spoke, knowing that most of the world's people spoke more than one, everyone that is, except the American.

"Bola, have you ever been to England or any other country?" I asked.

"Oh no, sir. I have never left this country. I only want to go to America someday because I hear it's really something."

I took a guess that Bola was in his mid thirties, and although we might have been the same age, he looked much older. From the looks of things here I could see why he would get older faster. Would I age the same way if I lived here? In thinking about that I almost had an anxiety attack. To calm myself down I tried to think of a tune. I also wondered what Bola would have done had he met Ol' Jake and his boys in America. Would he still feel the same about my country? Did he know what it was like to be terrorized every day of his life? He wouldn't have read that in any book, that the black man in America lived his whole life in terror. My search for freedom in Africa was to get away from that torture, and Bola had dreams of going toward it. In many instances, in traveling, I would make up a song. Most of the hits I wrote happened when I was traveling, but there was nothing here to motivate anything in me but sadness.

Part of my African dream was to be motivated to write a song with the original people of the drum. I had always been blown away by the rhythms of Africa, but so far all I saw was people crapping on the side of the road. What lyrics would I use in a song? About someone sitting on the road? About someone crapping? There's no way I could tell anybody this back home and have them believe me, let alone have them believe that people shit in the street.

"What kind of diseases do these people get from it?" I asked Bola. "Are there any medical facilities, hospitals for the sick? There must be a lot of people dying."

"There are some hospitals, but they are not worth going to, sir."

"That's hard to believe," I said. "Not worthy of going to?"

I knew back home they wouldn't believe that either, or that there were tribes called Niggers and Sam-Bo's. We'd been called that for so long, in such a negative way, that it would be hard for them to believe that those names had a royal attachment. The black American had such fear of those names that it would take damn near an act from God to convince them that they were names to be proud of. The average black American probably would think that I'd gone to Africa and completely lost my mind.

In a way, maybe I did. What I found, I wasn't looking for, and what I was looking at, I still can't believe it. Watching monkeys climb trees would've made more sense. Even if I stayed and lived among these people a natural lifetime I don't think I could ever feel close enough to fit in and be what I thought I was, an African man. If anything, the most I could ever be is a man from Africa. It took me going all the way to Africa to realize that what I truly am, is a black American.

20
How the White Man Lucked Up

During my ride to the hotel, I pondered the words nigger and sambo, and came to the conclusion that probably through the confusion of teaching slaves a new language, the words were used because the white man had no other names for black slaves. We were from Africa and that's all he knew about us. He said what he knew: niggers and sambo, and you'd have to use your imagination a little and think how people spoke four hundred years ago on this land we call America. We might have been from tribes that sounded like nigger and sambo, so that's what he called us.

There was nothing here then, so slave traders and owners used what they knew best. But, I think he lucked up when he realized those names could humiliate the slave. This was when the slaves began to learn the meaning of his master's words, especially if they came with a crack on the head with a stick. I'm sure the beatings were the white man's way of getting his point across. You know, kind of how they do now, except today they use a gun to get our attention.

When the white man discovered the word nigger was as powerful as his stick, and that it was safer for him not to use that stick, he put it down and used the word with just as much effectiveness. I clearly understand what happened to my forefathers. Each time they were beaten and called a bad nigger, it took a subconscious toll on them as being something bad, so they feared it. I believe that's where the term, "No boss, I ain't no nigger," came from, because it was associated with pain.

Something else was mighty strange about this homecoming. I had not seen one single white person. That was amazing to me. In all this mass of humanity there had to be tens of thousands of dollars of commerce and I had not seen one white trader anywhere. Is that why the country was so messed up? Wherever there's commerce there had to be traders. All the traders I had ever seen were white, so I asked.

"Are there any other people here besides Africans, Bola? You know, not just us black folk, but white people?"

"Oh yes sir. The British are the rulers of this country and there are plenty of French and Belgians. Lebanese and Chinese are also here. If they weren't, we'd probably still be bush people. There are other foreigners running the infrastructure of this country as well, building roads, and most of the businesses and commerce, but the people are governed by the soldiers.

"Everything is done by the foreigners," he continued. "They import the food, drill for the oil, control the shipping and banking, and unless you're in the army, you work for them. We natives have only small businesses, and we buy from what they bring in to sell at the market. The big chiefs are the ones who bring the foreigners here, because we're told that we are nothing but a bunch of illiterates."

"Who are these big chiefs, and why do they have so much power?" I asked.

"Traditionally they are well educated and from rich families, and they're mayors of the same villages, generation after generation," said Bola. "They succeed each other, buy all the goods from the foreigners, and sell it to us and get richer. Simple people don't have a chance. Those chiefs don't care too much for the little people, unless of course, you're a close relative."

So there wasn't much difference between here and the way things were done back in America. Actually, there wasn't a difference at all. Well, maybe one. The difference here is it's black on black. In America, it's white on white. It is amazing that the chiefs, who crowned themselves as indigenous traders, mayors, educators, and town keepers still let the heart of the country, such as banking, shipping, and trading, run through white channels. That was normal *in Africa*!

Everybody who's poor believes in that pie in the sky over there, but how can a person see it's falling when they are down on their knees asking for it? With my little pea brain I know that wasn't it. The powerful have never given the powerless anything but more pain.

Also, I couldn't understand why there were so many people on their knees praying with their heads down in Africa when they should be looking up. So far I'd seen as much of that as I'd seen crapping on the ground. I wondered if being on our knees was the universal way the white man taught us to be robbed in prayer? All of this was the way we were told to keep the faith, by prayer, and good things would come if we kept our heads down and on our knees, and believed in miracles.

Meanwhile the big man, the boss man, the white man, is the Chinaman, the Lebanese, and the Frenchman, all digging in the ground for gold and oil. Now I believe in faith and prayer, but I strongly felt that these people needed to get up off the ground and off their knees, put a shovel in their hands and get busy. Do exactly what we are doing as black Americans. I honestly believe that one can move mountains, as long as he begins by carrying away small stones. I do believe that. I didn't create the problems, but I do believe you can't pray all of them away. You have to move them. The same as if you had to run out of a burning house. Praying won't stop the fire.

The two-hour ride into Lagos was interesting, and what I saw along the way will last a lifetime in my memory. If I could, I thought, I would take Bola back to America with me, as I thought he was good man and trustworthy, dedicated to his job. I felt he was an honest person, too. He called himself small, but he had no idea how big he was in my eyes and I hoped he'd see his dream fulfilled, as I had seen mine. When we got to the hotel, I thanked him for the ride, and paid him fifty dollars without knowing that could've been a half-year's worth of salary.

I now think about how many black people in America will never get a chance to know a man like Bola, to have a little chat and have that experience of being with another black person two worlds apart. It was so amazing. We looked alike but knew nothing about each other. It is very important that black Americans travel. You'll be surprised at what you find, especially when it comes to knowing who you are and the history about your past. We have been downgraded so long it may be hard to find a way back. Yes, it can be difficult to look up, but don't be afraid or apologetic. Just start looking and you'll find a way.

The black American also needs to know they can stick their chests out and be proud when someone calls them a Nigger or Sambo. It seems all races of people around the world think they're above the American black. No, it's not so. Don't believe it. Personally speaking, I'm honored to be a black man. Do you know how wonderful it is to be one of a kind? I'll take that all day. And, I believe our race is part of the bigger plan, and that God had everything to do with it. There's nowhere on earth I can go and not be seen as one of the most recognizable images on the planet. Talk about iconic? It's the black face. I'd love nothing better than to walk up to a skinhead, shake his hand and say, "Hi, I'm a Nigger. Who are you?"

I imagine those of us right out of Africa were a real confused bunch when we got to America. All we knew was what we were taught. We had been taken to a strange land and whatever the master wanted us to know, that's what he told us. Even being called by our own names was frightening, once he controlled us.

I'll bet that's when it was all hell, trying to get us to understand him. I suppose it was like talking to a dog. You tell the dog to come and he barks and wags his tail. Do you know what he's saying when he does that? No, so you take a stick and whip his butt until you think he understands. That's what it was like with the whites towards the blacks. Back then they had to have their way with us. But how could we possibly have understood them? I don't understand them now. When he said God created man in his own image, was it to justify his madness? The earth god with all his genius, I have to say he's still sumdumhonky.

21
The Federal Palace Hotel

One thing was for certain, Bola wasn't lying about how grand the hotel was. We drove through a huge main gate and up a circled driveway where there were many little stands with people selling everything from American candies to whole ivory tusks. At first glance it looked like they had goods from all around the world right there in the yard of the hotel. It was very clean, and the men at the stands were all called Alhaji, or that's what I thought they were called. It all even seemed kind of civil.

Walking into the lobby, I rated the hotel itself among the best I'd been in. The check-in desk was in the heart of a beautiful marble circle with a giant chandelier over it. Everyone was in uniform, from the manager to the doorman, and I was really impressed. This was the stuff I had envisioned, and it was beginning to look like something to come home for. A nice lady with a big, broad smile named Mary checked me in. She really looked good, like someone you'd see in New York, in a disco club, and you couldn't wait to get a dance with her. Actually, I could hardly take my eyes off of her, even though she didn't speak English.

"Mr. Price," she said, "do you have any naira . . . our money?"

"No," I said.

"Then I will exchange your dollars for naira, okay?"

I was thinking the exchange rate would be like in Korea or Japan, where with just a few hundred dollars you'd need a box to carry around the stuff. I had no reason to think otherwise. Looking at the surroundings and conditions I'd just passed through, I thought a few dollars here would be like a blood transfusion for the country.

"What's the exchange rate?" I asked.

"Two dollars for one naira," she replied sweetly.

"What?"

"Yes, that is the rate and the rate for your room per night is one hundred and fifty."

"You mean three hundred a night? Madam, you're telling me that your naira has more value than the American dollar?"

"Yes, something like that."

"It costs as much to sleep here as it costs at the Waldorf?"

"This is our Waldorf, sir. We just call it the Federal Palace Hotel. Now, you're going to be with us how long, sir?"

"I'm not sure now," I said.

"Okay then," she said, "leave one thousand US dollars on deposit. If you stay longer we will ring your room to notify you that the money is out. Okay, sir?"

Still a little dazed over the cost, I nodded.

The bellhop took me to the elevator, which should've been a warning, but I paid little attention. My room was on the tenth floor and the ride up was like being flushed through a sewage pipe at Madison Square Garden during a Muhammad Ali championship fight night. I tried to hold my breath for ten floors, to avoid that funky polyester and dried fish smell. It was an odor worse than an open septic tank and I was sure there was no deodorant known to man that would kill it. I had never smelled a dead body, but it couldn't have been any worse.

Luckily, my room turned out to be quite nice. It was no Waldorf, but it was okay. I wanted to get the funk off my body from that elevator ride, so my first stop was the bathtub. There was a super big tub with fixtures that looked like gold, and two large beds. I knew this would be my spot for a while. After dodging those funk bullets, I needed a bath, and decided to do just that. But, when I turned on the faucet, nothing came out. I thought maybe I'd turned on the wrong valve, but there was only one. No water? Finally I called the front desk.

"No, sir. There is no water now, but it will come soon," I was told.

"How long?" I asked. "Oh, I don't know, sir, but it will come soon."

I accepted "come soon" as being something reasonable. Why not? Shit happens. Maybe I should try some food? No answer at room service. My third choice was to look through the double glass doors of the patio off my room, and there was the Atlantic Ocean. For as far as I could see, the ocean was beautiful. It wasn't like I hadn't seen the ocean before, but the splendor of the sun setting on the water blew me away, and that moment brought to mind the history of times gone by. I could almost see the slave ships leaving the port, some carrying members of my lost family in chains, raw hard nails in their lips, and no clothing.

After that great moment of tragic thought, I noticed to my right a bunch of shanties with smoke coming out of them so heavily that I thought something was on fire. Then I saw a flag and some soldiers, and thought what I was looking at might be some kind of military camp, and it was. It was a camp built right in the inlet, off and around the hotel. That's nice, I thought, the hotel was in a good spot.

I then spotted another building, this one in the circle of the hotel's lagoon. That building, I later found, was a refreshment center. And, beyond that beautiful setting was a wall built around the lagoon to keep the water out of the hotel. Fair enough, I thought. I went through all of that to say that on top of that wall, there must have been fifty big, fat bare asses hanging over it dropping shit for the world to see. Each ass was aimed directly at the patio of the Federal Palace Hotel. If I had anything to compare it to, it would be like a bunch of birds sitting on a wire taking an afternoon shit.

That upset me at first, then I realized I shouldn't be upset, because it was their country, not my mine. I figured the best thing for me to do, while I waited for the water to come back on, was to see what was on television, and let them shit in peace. I turned the switch, lay on the bed, and waited for about five minutes. No picture. No sound. I thought the plug was not connected, but that wasn't it. Three hundred a day and the damn television didn't work either.

"Hello, front desk."

I tried to keep my voice down and stay calm, but what an effort it was. "What the hell's going on here? The damn television doesn't work."

"Oh, sir, I'm so sorry," the voice at the other end said, "but this morning the NNPA (the National Nigerian Power Authority) took away the lights."

For a second he had me.

"Look," I said again, "my television doesn't work."

"I know sir, there's nothing I can do about it. NNPA took away the lights, we just have to wait."

"And who the hell is NNPA?"

"Sir, that is the National Nigerian Power Authority. When they're working on the lines, the lights come and go."

So what was I supposed to do? I couldn't help think about all the other foreigners in the hotel who might be having the same kind of experience I was having. I couldn't imagine anybody coming back here for a repeat visit. What a home coming this was turning out to be. Not one thing had gone right, except the ride with Bola.

There was a time when I thought that finding my way back to Africa was next to impossible, but I was wrong. Here I was! But I didn't think I was wrong about the impossible task of being able to find the village of my family, or where in Africa that might be. Which was the tribe I came from? Even if I found my village, what would I say to the people there? I don't speak their language and they don't speak mine. How will they know me? What is it about me that says I'm African? And, with no marks on my face, who and what am I to them?

Then it dawned on me. My ancestors were so long gone from my roots of Africa that I was about as much an African as I am Chinese. I also never even considered that after four hundred years that I could have had many ancestors from many villages and many tribes.

For people of my kind there was no trace of language that had been handed down from generation to generation, so there was no homeland for me other than the place of my birth. One thing was for sure. I was certainly not African. I found that out immediately and took it seriously. However, when it came to finding my home grounds and the origin of my family's birthplace I came to believe that would be best left to a dream, as time and each generation had eroded all of that as if it never was. No recollection, no information, no ability to recall. That part of my history was dead.

I wasn't going to worry about it, though, and thought I'd just wait on NNPA, because there was nothing else I could do anyway. But while sitting there, a simple thought did cross my mind. Why should I be worried about this when we blacks in America have been in the dark so long that we can't see, even when the lights are on? I should at least be grateful, because my eyes were now open, and I knew that somewhere in my past I had a connection to Africa, even if the connection was nothing more than the color of my skin.

These Africans are the people of my past. What opened my eyes even wider was seeing all the suffering and misery here, which made it easier to understand the physical and emotional pain we all suffer in America. It was becoming more than obvious that we blacks came from a very strong bloodline, and that we were very, very special. So, I decided I was just going to sit there and use some of my Nigger and Sambo strength and wait on the lights and water to come back on. At three hundred a day, wouldn't you wait, too?

While I waited, I remembered when I was a kid I wondered where exactly in Africa I came from, and that I made up names for the boats my ancestors must have traveled on.

The one problem I always had was which part of Africa, and when did they leave? On this vast continent, even folks with the greatest minds would find it very difficult to pin point a particular spot. I think if you tried to figure it out the closest you'd get would be the boat, because the boats had names. If you knew all the facts and the names, you would still have problems, as the people were all picked up on different shores and sailed in the bottom of the boat with all tribes mixed as one. The only thing for sure was that we all didn't come from the same place.

The turning point came for my dream when I realized that completing my mission would be impossible. Can you imagine your forefathers leaving a continent blindfolded and shackled, and then you wake up one morning centuries later, put on your Nikes, and say I'm going home to Africa just as blind as my ancestors were when they left?

For most of my life that was my dream, and I expected everything to be fine when I got here. No one ever said what to expect, other than my primary teachers. I guess in my mind I was thinking it would be like New York, even though my teacher, Miss Brown, said Africans were all little pig-men who would eat you. I should have known there were no great big cities like New York in Africa.

When I was a kid I also often wondered how I'd get to Africa. I remember hearing my elders sing *Swing low, sweet chariot, it's coming for to carry me home*. Somewhere in my mind that's what that song always meant to me. A chariot was going to take me home, but my chariot ended up being a Boeing DC 10. It was not what I expected, not even remotely close, but I had lived my vision, and the mystique was gone.

It wasn't until the next morning that NNPA turned on the electricity at the Federal Palace, and it was a few hours after that when the water came on. I was so pissed I wanted my three hundred bucks a day back, and to tell that little pretty lady named Mary that she should never mention this place and the Waldorf in the same breath. But, I was too funky by then to leave the room or do anything other than bathe. The bath did nothing to cool me off, though, because the water that came out of the faucet was almost as hot as the temperature outside, and nether did it help the smell. That was forever in the air.

22
Africa

I realized very quickly that going from Kenner, Louisiana to Africa was not like going from Kenner to another part of Louisiana, like to a cousin's house in the country, for example. If I thought an African would accept me because I looked like him, then I was mistaken and needed to think that over again. I had another thought, too. Just being in Africa didn't make me African. It didn't take long to find out that the world of reality and the world of my dreams were in two different places. The Africans were the first to let me know that because I am black it does not mean I was accepted, and as such, I could have easily been one of my redneck cousins. As far as they were concerned, to them I was an American.

I'm not a person who takes anything for granted, but I believed I was African for most of my life, up until I actually went there. Plus, there were mirrors in our house. I could see what I looked like. Ol' Jake and his people also said I was, and I said so all my life. So I believed it. I also heard it in the 'hood so I wasn't alone in thinking I was an African man. There was a street corner in Kenner where the tell-a-nigger tell–a-gram press hung out. It was inside the 'hood's barbershop and everybody knew everything, and they believed we were all African, too.

Although that "we from Africa" stuff did have some validity, I must say it had an affect on me. I still don't know the first thing about being an African, even though I ended up living there for a while. But, I never lived as an African. The only way I knew how to live was like a white man in America. I never lived in a mud hut, or a village, and other than that one night in the hotel, I can't ever remember being without lights. Before that trip I don't think I knew what I felt or who I was. So in that sense, the trip did me well.

Bemused, perplexed, and in a sense bewildered, I didn't understand any of this life in Africa, other than the fact that Africans are resilient people. Slave masters thought for sure after almost five centuries that there'd be none left of us, those who came to America on little wooden boats. What is more perplexing is that he didn't believe when he saw the strength of the African. He figured with the bad food he fed them, for sure they couldn't last long. But, here it is hundreds of years later and we are still here and growing.

The only American history about the great strength of my people that I had heard about is how many got hung. What confuses me is that there was a whole continent of Africans who knew the struggle that went with the slave trading of their brothers, and there's no record of any of them, where they tried to help. Why is it with every important event that has brought change to man there's a history that has been written by the white man? There is no true documentation of my ancestors from Africa.

The white man wanted us to be like him, and even though he didn't treat us well, he did make history. He totally changed us from a people of the soil. He stripped us of our land, culture, identity, and rhythms in ways we will never know again. Wouldn't it have been something had he been able to change our color, too? He totally changed our way of thinking so we could be like him, and he gave us a new voice.

We have his needs, his likes, and dislikes. We have his aspirations and desires. What a great "accomplishment," being able to change another man's ideas and ways of life to suit your personal needs. The only other time this happened was with the Native Americans, and look how that turned out for them.

After Columbus went to North America the white man discovered that this Indian son-bitch was smart. He could kill a buffalo for dinner, take his hide to build himself a house, and make clothes with it, too. He used the buffalo skin for his musical instruments, to make strings for his bows, and a hammock for his bed. Then on top of that there were no taxes, no rent, and he had families and communities. Who were these people who had such a perfect system? Here's an untitled poem to describe how I would've seen it:

Columbus wanted to take this to the queen!
He got so excited.
"For sure I'll be knighted."
With tears in his throat. Wait!
Can this land float?
He conceived a plan to just take land.
"I'll hitch it to the back of my boat."

Filled with glee. "Oh lucky, lucky me,
All I need is some hitch and rope.
Tie the land to a winch at the back of the boat,
And out to sea, set the best sail to float."
But then came a storm,
and many of his vessels were gone.
He fought for his life, though wet of the storm.
It was no joke.
Up pop some red folk to see exactly
what was going on.
"Oh my, my, What shall I do?
I've lost my vessels and half of my crew."
And two summers had passed, really, really fast
The only food to eat was meat and grass
The few men were left were pretty close to death
They were so thin and frail.
Times was rough, the winters were tough
Columbus himself looked fractured and pale.
He tried to forget that his mission had failed,
But he went on to get ready to sail.
Enough of this bubble.
Men before had struggled.
Let no one know of our trouble?
"Ahoy, oh captain," one shipmate say
"Two years on the waters, no mention of pay?"
Columbus, a man who wants to be knighted
And to have the Queen's blessings,
this fault must be righted.
He thought for a moment then said to the crew.
"This might be cynical, but here's what we'll do.
Money and fame I'll give you in crocks,

But what happened here, you will say not.
To your brother, your wife, not even each other.
We will just lie, and say we found this land.
We discovered!"
But Columbus had to figure this whole thing out.
The red man was a problem he could do without
Every question had answers, and this one did too.
Why not befriend these bush men?
Yes, that's what we'll do.
Let's give them whisky and chocolates
to tickle their feathers,
Maybe we'll get to know them a little bit better.
They may tell us the name of this place
we don't know
And a way back to Spain to set sail when we go?
"Ahoy, oh captain, I admire your view.
But, if we take the land, do we take them too?
These men with feathers and long horse hair,
What will you say to the queen
when we get them there?
How would you describe this land,
so far from the East?
And what do you say of people
who live like the beast?"
Columbus said, "This is not out of hand.
We'll do what we do when we find other land.
To hell with matters, we'll just stake our claim,
And these men with feathers,
we'll just give them a name.
There's the German, Frenchman, Irishman,
and Jew,

The Englishman, Roman, and Chinaman, too.
Spain has might and power galore.
She stretches her arms from shore to shore.
And within these valleys so vast, so plain,
We'll tell the queen we found the red man.
And to cause the queen no embarrassment,
Let's just tell the court and the queen where we went
To a land like Spain, maybe twice her size,
And she can send her troops there to colonize."

That brings me back to this point. Am I to believe the largest continent on earth had nothing but slaves on it, and all Europeans had to do was go there and pick them like up apples? What else were they looking for? Did they befriend them with whiskey and chocolates, and what was in those treats to have them give up their sons and daughters, and their way of life they had lived from the beginning of time? Was it diamonds, plutonium, and gold? And the only suitable character they found to write about, in a belittled way, was their own handling of the nigger? Great events in time are researched and written, but where is the African man's true history?

23
Awakening

Many years have gone by since the height of my career, and since I went to Africa, and a lot of the people I knew are gone, too. I suppose that's just the way it is. But there's one evil that will always be and that's some men's cruelty toward others. I probably won't ever understand it, but I must admit that I had it backward for a long time, that is until I went to Africa.

Before then I didn't think any man on earth could be as mean to another man as that honky was to black men in America, and I mean all shades of black. No matter what they called themselves if you weren't a redneck it was mercy, mercy. It wasn't until John F. Kennedy ran for president and spoke of injustice that other nations began to know that many American white men had no compassion at all for black folks or people of color.

It wasn't only economics, but the pain and hurt and suffering that he inflicted on us. The white man would probably still be the MF he really is if not for John F. Kennedy, who pulled the cover off him. When he became president he was not that high on mixing, but to call it to the attention of the nation may have cost him his life, and that was enough to put it all in its proper perspective. Niggers learned a lot from that. One lesson for sure was stand up, and not tolerate brutality, and many of us died because of our new stance. We also learned there's no peace without blood.

But even then that didn't stop the honky. Some went on national TV and declared in the name of God that a black person to him was not human, and that there was no power on Earth that would make him treat us as though we were. Because of his disgraceful ways, hundreds of us suffered and died shameful deaths, but even that didn't buy his respect, as his policemen still shot us in the street like wild dogs.

I'm sure every time he closed his eyes he begged for forgiveness for the nights he sat up plotting how to get rid of us, his one true "friend," the black man, his cousin and son. How alone he must feel now in the twenty-first century with people of all colors surrounding him from everywhere, and most of them he has pissed off.

Yet as bad as he was and is, he's nowhere near as bad as that in-house nigger who we called "Tom," "black gangster," or "rat." As far as blacks were concerned, he was more dangerous than that white man could ever be. The nigger who sat at your dinner table, called you brother, swallowed your every word along with your food then sold you out for peanuts, is the real dog. I'll bet anything that the word "sing" came from that "Uncle Tom."

He was then, and is now, the one who will "go and tell it on the mountain." Whatever the agenda, whatever the news out in the yard, he'd go inside and tell it to the master. The white man didn't get information from the cotton field;

he got it from the nigger in the kitchen. That process got many brothers killed.

I'm sure by now you know the term "my nigger." That's not an imagination. That SOB is real. Don't fall asleep when he is around. He is still out there and you will have to watch your back.

Before I close, I want to share with you my two of my biggest lifelong confusions. First, I thought the way we were treated in this country by the white man was terrible and sinful, so unforgiving that I almost thought that the honky was the devil. And second, the white man preached all that "up to heaven and down to hell" crap until most of us feared every word, along with lightning and thunder when it rained. I don't need to remind you that death is death, no matter how it comes, and although the white man has nothing to do with wherever it is you or I end up, he certainly had us afraid of dying by telling us where we were going.

Still, I must say the white man was a master at marketing his stories. It takes a whole lot of big balls to tell a son-bitch you know which way he's going after he dies if he doesn't obey you. I used to think he was a black man's worst nightmare —'til I went to Africa.

24
And Then I Went Home

God has blessed me in many ways. One of my greatest blessings was being snatched from Kenner and being allowed to play my music. Why was that? Was it because God had seen fit to save me from those evil men? Or, was it the way I honored my mother and father? They really were the true heroes in my life and when they called on me I was ready to serve. Is that why?

It was not my hope to become who I am. The only thing I really wanted for myself was peace for my parents. They were good, loving, hard-working people who sacrificed everything to take care of their eleven children and help anyone else they could. Was that why young folks fell in love with my music? Or, was it when my dad broke his hip that I really heard my parents' cry for help, and that's when my life started to change?

Then, out of nowhere I began to feel a stronger sense of commitment to my parents, and I believe that's what inspired me to write songs like "Lawdy Miss Clawdy." I just could not bear to see them suffer, and the best blessing I got from that song was that my parents never had to work again. That song fulfilled my every dream.

Some forty odd years ago when I first went to the Motherland the excitement I felt was almost too much to take. I wanted Africa like a junkie needed a fix. Most of my life I just knew there had to be someplace in the world where a black man could feel free in his mind and in his spirit.

In America, everywhere I turned there was an Ol' Jake watching us at every turn with that big brother, I spy I got my eye on you boy, bullshit. Africa had to be a relief. America had gotten to be much more than a man with any pride and a will to live could stand. Many times I asked myself how much more? Fear of this man gave us an abundance of stress and I would imagine that is one reason why high blood pressure is almost an epidemic among black people.

I'm still having the hardest time trying to figure out why some men are so inhumane to others. For most of my life I thought it was a black and white thing, probably because that's what I saw growing up being a second-class citizen. It almost seemed natural the way we were treated in America. But I can tell you now, without

"Lloyd Price has been the ultimate survivor. Nearly six decades after the milestone 'Lawdy Miss Clawdy,' he hasn't shown signs of slowing down. He has mastered both entertainment and the business world, and he'll always be remembered as one of the true pioneers and forerunners of rock 'n' roll music."
—Examiner.com

hesitation, what Africans do to Africans make our black and white crap look like child's play. There's no way you could see Africa the way I saw it and not ask yourself, does one African male have any human spirit at all toward another, let alone have any commitment to human ideals?

The Africans I saw did not live that spiritual ideal that commits you to law, order, and leadership. Even though that white man came from the caves, he was smart enough to know that life works better with order.

And that's the last thing I will talk about. Order. With all the abuse we took, there was some order in it. Looking back, there was always a structure in the white man's organization. It made no difference if he came in cars or on horses, one dozen or one, it was organized. To make myself clear, if that honky came to get you it was because he thought you had broken one of his laws, or the house nigger I talked about ratted on you and said you did. It was no secret how he felt about us. He was very honest about letting us know his feelings that there was nothing a black man could do to make himself equal to him.

According to the white earth god, whites and blacks had nothing in common, so if a black man allegedly did something out of order you could be sure a honky would get a group of his buddies to enforce the order of the law that he wrote. He didn't pretend to be your brother or your friend. That's the difference.

In Africa there is absolutely no such law and order, spiritual or otherwise. There it's black on black. Their inhumanity toward each other is so much greater that it makes you wonder how a man could look like you, have the same cultural background, speak in the same tongue, live off the same land that God gave each of us, and over some stupid mistake or attitude catch one of your neighbor's sons or daughters and hack them to pieces. Or, catch someone's wife or husband and put a tire over their heads and douse them with gasoline and burn them alive. Or maybe have a group of thugs come to your village and beat your family in the head with rocks until they bled to death, and if they find you, take you to the ocean, chop you up alive and feed you to the fish piece by piece. Or how about this: one morning you wake up and find your village burned to the ground and your house is the only one standing. And, it's all some political fight to make your people think you burned down the village. Then, without any kind of a hearing, they grab you for justice. It could cost you an arm and a leg right there on the spot without any due judgment and to top that, for your whole life you've worked for less than a dollar a day. That's if you were lucky enough to stay alive and not get hit on the road before you turn frothy with some illness.

When I was in Africa, no one knew what a speed limit, stop sign, or a red light was. If you got hit by a speeding vehicle the driver would keep going and let you lie there suffering from your injury until you died. Worse than that, did you know that no one will touch you, because if they do, they will become responsible for your burial? So your body will be there until you rot and burst wide open from the heat, and the stench will be unbearable. Insects and animals will eat off of you until, somewhere in the night, someone might throw the remains of your body in the water. Then the water will become full of unknown diseases, cholera, e-coli, and don't forget AIDS.

▲

It's been a long time since then and the world is changing. Finally, things are happening in my lifetime that I thought just a few years ago would never happen. Each generation is bringing about a change and I notice in the Motherland, in Africa, there are fewer political coups and people are trying to get along to bring some order to all that madness. Being educated helps, as does being smarter about life, too.

Our cousins are even nicer on this side of the ocean. Is it because there's a half human, half white man as president in the White House? Millions of people said he was the best man for that job not once, but twice, and many of my old, bald-headed white cousins say he's the worst man ever to sit in that chair. Five centuries have passed and that white man is still out there bitching.

I am here to tell you, that is some sumdumhonky! But don't forget, he's watching. He is always watching.

THE END

Discography*

***some overseas and compilation releases, and CD and vinyl re-releases not listed**

Albums

Lloyd Price	Specialty	1959
Mr. Personality	ABC-Paramount	1959
The Exciting Lloyd Price	ABC-Paramount	1959
Mr. Personality's 15 Big Hits	ABC-Paramount	1960
Mr. Personality Sings the Blues	ABC-Paramount	1960
The Fantastic Lloyd Price	ABC-Paramount	1960
Cookin' with Lloyd Price	ABC-Paramount	1961
Lloyd Price Sings the Million Sellers	ABC-Paramount	1961
Misty	Double-L	1963
This is My Band	Double-L	1963
Mr. Rhythm & Blues	Grand Prix	1964
Come to Me	Guest Star	1964
Lloyd Swings for Sammy	Monument	1965
Big Hits	Pickwick	1967
Lloyd Price Now!	Turntable	1969
To the Roots and Back	GSF	1972
The Best of Lloyd Price	Scepter/Citation	1972
16 Greatest Hits	ABC	1972
Lloyd at Any Price	Joy	1974
Music—Music	LPG/Don	1976
The Nominee	Olde World	1978
Walkin' the Track	Specialty	1986
Here Comes the Night	NFS	1987
Guest Star Records Presents	Guest Star	Unk.
Vintage Gold	MCA	1988
Lloyd Price	Bellaphon	1988
Greatest Hits	MCA	1988
Lloyd Price: Greatest Hits	MCA	1989
Personality Plus	Specialty	1990
Lloyd Price Greatest Hits	Curb	1990
Stagger Lee	Collectables	1992
Lloyd Price Vol. 2: Heavy Dreams	Specialty	1993
Lloyd Price Sings his Big Ten	Curb	1994

Greatest Hits: The Original	ABC Paramount/MCA	1994
Lawdy Miss Clawdy	Ace	1995
Body with No Body	Moms	1998
Mr. Personality	Sba	1999
The Exciting Lloyd Price	Sba	1999
Christmas Classics	Prestige	2002
20th Century Presents The Best of Lloyd Price: The Millennium Collection	Universal	2002
Classics: 1952-1953	Nad	2004
Lawdy!	Fantasy	2005
Speciality Profiles	Specialty	2006
The Great Lloyd Price	Goldies	2006
16 Greatest Hits	Passport Audio	2006
Golden Legends: Lloyd Price	Madacy	2006
I'm Feeling Good: Standards in Swing	Big Deal	2012
Lawdy Miss Clawdy	Blue Label	2007
The Exciting Lloyd Price + Mr. "Personality"	Hoodoo	2010

Charted Releases

Lawdy Miss Clawdy	#1 R&B	1952
Oooh-Oooh-Oooh	#4 R&B	1952
Restless Heart	#5 R&B, flip of above	1952
Ain't it a Shame?	#4 R&B	1953
Tell Me Pretty Baby	#8 R&B, flip of above	1953
Just Because	#3 R&B, #29 Pop	1957
Lonely Chair	#88 Pop	1957
Stagger Lee Certified Gold	#1 R&B, #1 Pop, UK #7	1959
Where Were You (On Our Wedding Day?)	#4 R&B, #23 Pop, UK #15	1959
Personality Certified Gold	#1 R&B, #2 Pop, UK #9	1959
I'm Gonna Get Married Certified Gold	#1 R&B, #3 Pop, UK #23	1959
Three Little Pigs	#15 R&B, flip of above	1959
Come Into My Heart	#2 R&B, #20 Pop	1960
Wont'cha Come Home flip of above	#6 R&B, #43 Pop	1960

"Lady Luck"	#3 R&B, #14 Pop	1960
"Never Let Me Go"	#26 R&B, #82 Pop	1960
"No If's – No And's"	#16 R&B, #40 Pop	1960
"For Love"	#43 Pop	1960
"Question"	#5 R&B, #19 Pop	1960
Just Call Me and I'll Understand	#79 Pop	1960
Who Coulda' Told You They Lied	#103 Pop	1960
You Better Know What You're Doin'	#90 Pop	1961
Mary and Man-O	#110 Pop	1961
Under Your Spell Again	#123 Pop	1962
Misty	#11 R&B, #21 Pop	1963
Billie Baby	#84 Pop	1964
I Love You I Just Love You	#123 Pop	1964
Amen	#124 Pop	1964
If I Had My Life to Live Over	#107 Pop	1965
Bad Conditions	#21 R&B	1969
Trying to Slip Away	#32 R&B	1973
What Did You Do With My Love	#99 R&B	1976
I'm Feeling Good: Standards in Swing (album)	#11 Billboard Jazz	2013

Singles

Lawdy Miss Clawdy / Mailman Blues	Specialty	1952
Oooh-Oooh-Oooh / Restless Heart	Specialty	1952
Ain't It a Shame? / Tell Me Pretty Baby	Specialty	1953
What's the Matter Now / So Long	Specialty	1953
Where You At / Baby Don't Turn Your Back On Me	Specialty	1953
I Wish Your Picture Was You / Frog Legs	Specialty	1953
Let Me Come Home Baby / Too Late For Tears	Specialty	1954
Walkin' the Track Jimmie Lee	Specialty	1954
Chee-Koo Baby / Oo-Ee Baby	Specialty	1954
Gold Cadillac Song (one-sided single)	Specialty	1954
Trying to Find Someone to Love / Lord, Lord, Amen!	Specialty	1955
Woe Ho Ho / I Yi Yi Gomen-A-Sai (I'm Sorry)	Specialty	1956

Country Boy Rock / Rock 'N' Dance	Specialty	1956
Forgive Me, Clawdy / I'm Glad	Specialty	1956
Baby, Please Come Home / Breaking My Heart (All Over Again)	Specialty	1957
The Chicken and the Bop / Lonely Chair	KRC	1957
Hello Little Girl / Georgianna	KRC	1957
How Many Times / To Love and Be Loved	KRC	1957
Just Because / Why	KRC	1957
Oh, Oh, Oh / Mailman Blues	ABC-Paramount	1957
Stagger Lee / You Need Love	ABC-Paramount	1958
No Limit to Love / Such a Mess	KRC	1958
Down by the River	KRC	1958
Gonna Let You Come Back Home / Down By The River	KRC	1959
Lawdy Miss Clawdy / Mailman Blues	Specialty	1959
Where Were You (On Our Wedding Day)? / Is it Really Love?	ABC-Paramount	1959
(You've Got) Personality / Have You Ever Had the Blues	ABC-Paramount	1959
I'm Gonna Get Married / Three Little Pigs	ABC-Paramount	1959
Come Into My Heart / Wont'cha Come Home	ABC-Paramount	1959
Lady Luck / Never Let Me Go	ABC-Paramount	1960
No If's – No And's / For Love	ABC-Paramount	1960
Question / If I Look a Little Blue	ABC-Paramount	1960
Just Call Me (And I'll Understand) / Who Coulda' Told You (They Lied)	ABC-Paramount	1960
(You Better) Know What You're Doin' / That's Why Tears Come and Go	ABC-Paramount	1961
Boo Hoo / I Made You Cry	ABC-Paramount	1961
Say, I'm the One / One Hundred Percent	ABC-Paramount	1961
String of Pearls / Chantilly Lace	ABC-Paramlunt	1961
Mary and Man-O / I Ain't Givin' Up Nothin'	ABC-Paramount	1961
Talk to Me / I Cover the Waterfront	ABC-Paramount	1961
Be a Leader / 'Nother Fairy Tale	ABC-Paramount	1962

Twistin' the Blues / Pop Eye's Irresistible You	ABC-Paramount	1962
Misery / Come to Me	Curio	1962
Counterfeit Friends / Your Picture	ABC-Paramount	1962
Under Your Spell Again / Happy Birthday Mama	ABC-Paramount	1962
Feelin' Good / Cupid's Bandwagon	Ludix	1963
Who's Sorry Now / Hello Bill	ABC-Paramount	1963
Pistol Packin' Mama	Double-L	1963
Misty / Cry On	Double-L	1963
Merry Christmas Mama / Auld Lang Syne	Double-L	1963
You're Nobody Till Somebody Loves You / I'll Be a Fool for You	Double-L	1963
Billie Baby / Try a Little Bit of Tenderness	Double-L	1964
Don't Cry / I Love You (I Just Love You)	Monument	1964
Amen / I'd Fight the World	Monument	1964
Oh Lady Luck / Woman	Monument	1965
If I Had My Life to Live Over / Two for Love	Monument	1965
Go On Little Girl / You're Reading Me	Double-L	1965
Peeping and Hiding / Every Night	Double-L	1966
Send Me Some Loving / Somewhere Along the Way	Double-L	1966
Misty / Saturday Night	Hurd	1966
I Won't Cry Anymore / The Man Who Took the Valise Off the Floor of Grand Central Station at Noon	Reprise	1966
Just Because / Personality	ABC	1967
Luv. Luv, Luv / Take All	JAD	1968
Don't Stop Now / The Truth	JAD	1968
Bad Conditions	JAD	1969
I Understand / The Grass Will Sing (For You)	Turntable	1969
I Heard It Through The Grapevine / It's Your Thing	Turntable	1969
Bad Conditions / The Truth	Turntable	1969

Title	Label	Year
Lawdy Miss Clawdy / Little Volcano	Turntable	1969
Stagger Lee / Personality	ABC	1969
Ready for Betty / Beat in Trinidad	President	1970
Natural Sinner / Mr. and Mrs. Untrue	Scepter	1971
Hooked on a Feeling / If You Really Love Him	Scepter	1971
In the Eyes of God / The Legend of Nigger Charley	Paramount	1972
Sing a Song / Electric Lover	GSF	1972
Love Music / Just for Baby	GSF	1973
Trying to Slip (Away) / They Get Down	GSF	1973
Stagger Lee / (You've Got) Personality	MCA	1973
Lawdy Miss Clawdy	Specialty	1973
Where Were You (On Our Wedding Day) / Lady Luck	ABC Records	1973
Peppermint Twist / Stagger Lee	Scepter	1973
(You've Got) Personality	EMI Electrola	1973
Natural Sinner	Scepter	1974
Lady Luck / Never Let Me Go	Roulette	1974
Stagger Lee	President	1976
What Did You Do With My Love / Love Music	LPG Records	1976
For No Reason / Special Part of Me	Olde World	1977
Lawdy Miss Clawdy / I'm Gonna Get Married	Trip Oldies	1984
Heavy Dream / Operator	Specialty	1985
Stagger Lee / Just Because	Trip Oldies	1985
Personality / Three Little Pigs	Trip Oldies	1985
I Always Will / Street Love	NFS	1987
House That Thing / I'm Coming Back	NFS	1988
Stagger Lee '89 / Don't Pour	NFS	1989

EPs

Title	Label	Year
The Exciting Lloyd Price	ABC-Paramount	1959
Mr. Personality	ABC-Paramount	1960
Four Songs From Mr. Personality's Big Hits	ABC-Paramount	1960
Rockin' on 5th Ave* (*with Paul Anka)	ABC-Paramount	1961

Index

"The rock and roll movement of the mid-'50s had achieved its takeover of the music industry in just a few short years, and during that final year of the decade, no one was hotter than Lloyd Price."
–Way Back Attack

ABOUT THE AUTHOR

Lloyd Price was born in Kenner, Louisiana, on March 9, 1933. In the 1950s Lloyd dominated the *Billboard* charts, which was the beginning of a stellar music career. In addition, Lloyd partnered with Don King to distribute boxing events that were shown around the world, including Muhammad Ali's famed Rumble in the Jungle. Lloyd later developed affordable housing in New York, and erected forty-two townhouses in the Bronx. In 1993 Lloyd toured Europe with Jerry Lee Lewis, Little Richard, and Gary U.S. Bonds, and in 2005 he performed with fellow legends Jerry Butler, Gene Chandler, and Ben E. King as the "Four Kings of Rhythm and Blues." The concerts were recorded for a PBS television special and DVD. In 2010 Lloyd was inducted into the Louisiana Music Hall of Fame, and appeared and sang in the Season 1 finale of the HBO series *Treme*. Lloyd currently manages Icon Food Brands and a line of clothing and collectibles, and is working on *Lawdy Miss Clawdy*, a Broadway musical. In 1998, Lloyd Price was inducted into the Rock and Roll Hall of Fame.

READER AND BOOK CLUB QUESTIONS

1. How did Ol' Jake shape Lloyd's personality, and also his drive for success?
2. How would you have reacted to the same treatment from white adults that Lloyd received as a child? What would you have felt?
3. Lloyd's parents could not help him financially, but they did support his dream. How?
4. Why does Lloyd feel that education is so important? How could a higher education have helped him in his career?
5. At nineteen, how might you have reacted differently than Lloyd did to sudden fame?
6. Do you feel that Lloyd is justified in his feelings for certain Southern white men? Why or why not?
7. Do you think that the Nigeria that Lloyd describes in the 1970s still exists today? How might it have changed?
8. How have race relations in the United States changed since the time that Lloyd was a child?
9. At the top of his career, Lloyd and his band traveled by car. What other differences did you note in the life that Lloyd discusses throughout the book, versus life today?
10. Do you think the title of this book is a good one? Why or why not?
11. How will you view the world differently after having read *sumdumhonky*?
12. What is your favorite Lloyd Price song, and why?

Photo Credits

Cover photo: Jack Delano, photographer. "A cafe near the tobacco market." Durham, North Carolina, May 1940. Farm Security Administration - Office of War Information Photograph Collection (Library of Congress). LC-USF33- 020513-M2 [P&P]

Back Cover photos: Esther Bubly, photographer. "A sign at the Greyhound bus station." Rome, Georgia, September 1943. Farm Security Administration - Office of War Information Photograph Collection (Library of Congress). LC-USW3- 037939-E [P&P]

Door photo by Lisa Wysocky.

Author photo courtesy of Lloyd Price.

All interior photos courtesy of Lloyd Price unless otherwise noted.

Two-time US Olympian and world champion silver medalist Nick Symmonds is not your typical runner. He's short, he's stocky, and he's not afraid to speak up when he believes in a person or a cause. Nick has also consistently been at the top of the world rankings in the men's 800 meter for close to a decade. He is intense, passionate about his sport, and grounded. This small town boy is not anyone's typical idea of an activist or an international running sensation. But, he is both. Here, for the first time, Nick Symmonds brings readers intimately into his life, and candidly shares his greatest triumphs and his most challenging personal and professional struggles.

Eileen Moore, a Justice on the California Court of Appeal, presents a fresh comparison on gender biases that women face in film and within the US Supreme Court. From early stirrings of women's rights in 1848 in Seneca Falls, New York; through the pioneers of female equality, Moore delves into gender as no other author has before. Did movies foster the rights of women, or keep them harnessed to outdated roles? What about our legal system? How did our Supreme Court break the hearts of women, and then protect them? From workplace equality to women's rights, film and our legal system combined to both help and hinder American women.